MW01493619

Lisa—
Take time to
breathe and take care
of yourself!
Love—
Karen xo

P.S. Per the author:
"Please forgive editing errors!"

Also - check out the stories
on p. 102, p. 128, & p. 194!!

Powered by Me®
for Educators Pre-K to 12

The True Force behind all Classroom Strategies,
Higher Teaching Potential, and Student Progress.

SHERIANNA BOYLE

BALBOA.
PRESS

A DIVISION OF HAY HOUSE

Copyright © 2012 Sherianna Boyle Powered by ME®

All rights reserved. No part of this book may be used or reproduced by any means,
graphic, electronic, or mechanical, including photocopying, recording, taping or by any
information storage retrieval system without the written permission of the publisher
except in the case of brief quotations embodied in critical articles and reviews.

ISBN: 978-1-4525-6210-0 (sc)
ISBN: 978-1-4525-6212-4 (hc)
ISBN: 978-1-4525-6211-7 (e)

Library of Congress Control Number: 2012921244

Balboa Press books may be ordered through booksellers or by contacting:

Balboa Press
A Division of Hay House
1663 Liberty Drive
Bloomington, IN 47403
www.balboapress.com
1-(877) 407-4847

Because of the dynamic nature of the Internet, any web addresses or links contained in
this book may have changed since publication and may no longer be valid. The views
expressed in this work are solely those of the author and do not necessarily reflect the
views of the publisher, and the publisher hereby disclaims any responsibility for them.

The author of this book does not dispense medical advice or prescribe the use of any
technique as a form of treatment for physical, emotional, or medical problems without the
advice of a physician, either directly or indirectly. The intent of the author is only to offer
information of a general nature to help you in your quest for emotional and spiritual well-
being. In the event you use any of the information in this book for yourself, which is your
constitutional right, the author and the publisher assume no responsibility for your actions.

Any people depicted in stock imagery provided by Thinkstock are models,
and such images are being used for illustrative purposes only.
Certain stock imagery © Thinkstock.

Logo Design by Holly Rounseville, Logo Designer, MainstreetHost

Printed in the United States of America

Balboa Press rev. date: 10/29/2012

I dedicate the energy of this book to educators, parents, students, and families. Also to our three little mermaids.

ACKNOWLEDGMENTS

I feel incredibly blessed to have been guided and supported by the following individuals along this path. My mother, Judy Zradi and father Larry Zradi for all the sacrifices you made in order to provide me with the education and foundation I am so grateful for today. I love you both so much. To my husband, Kiernan Boyle; my soul mate, parenting partner, and most of all, my friend. Thank you for taking care of our girls to give me time to write. I love you. To my children; Megan, Mikayla, and Makenzie for the privilege of witnessing your life experiences. Your insight and wisdom of what it is like to be a child in education was one of the many propellers for this project. Megan thank you for the believe in you note you placed on my computer. Mikayla for showing me through your eagle eyes how to be present. Makenzie, thank you sweet girl, for supplying me with a sacred time nap time.

Cindy Horgan, my partner, friend and mentor who contributed her insight and stories to this book. Thank you for giving me the wings to fly. You are a treasure to the field of parenting and education.

Jueli Garfinkle my developmental editor. Thank you for helping me to see I had more inside me than I ever imagined. The imprint you have made on my life I will cherish forever. I am certain we will work together again. Mary Blair, my copy editor and yogi friend thank you for the time, commitment and energy you gave to this project. I will always be grateful for our connection.

Thank you Karen Maregni for sharing your third grade experiences, those students are lucky to have you. Sue Tilton for your free computer support, Mara Fornier for inviting me into your classroom, Gia Esquivel my original website designer which lead me to my vision. Holly Rounseville at MainstreetHost for your fabulous website creations. Thank you, Stefanie Patterson for your unselfish support and passion for supporting girls. I send out huge hugs to my friends and colleagues Lori Rush and Nancy Ashworth. My former principal Sharon Hartley, thank you for all the wonderful experiences at Station Avenue Elementary School and for reviewing this book. My friends Angela Church and Shauna Child's for cheering me on. Ana Zick for clearing my heart, literally.

Finally, to all of my students, thank you for shining your light and love on me these past ten years.

God Bless,
Sherianna

Contents

Chapter 6

Chapter 7

Chapter 8

About the Author

Sherianna Boyle, resides on Cape Cod, Massachusetts, with her husband and three daughters. She holds a Certificate of Advanced Graduate Study in School Psychology from The University of Massachusetts, Boston. Her background includes extensive work in the field of parent education, educational workshops, and she is a Professor of Psychology at Cape Cod Community College.

For the past ten years Sherianna has been teaching yoga and meditation. This includes a strong professional development in alternative approaches for anxiety, and the experience of owning and operating a yoga studio. In 2009, she branched into facilitating empowerment, community based workshops / resources for girls and young women. After six months of working on a curriculum she found her ideas and insight were capable of empowering not only girls but also the individuals supporting them. Sherianna shifted her focus, dedicating herself to writing, researching, and developing ways to support individuals in the educational community. Powered by Me® followed, a way to empower and connect students, teachers and families. Sherianna hopes to continue her journey educating about internal power through Powered by Me® books and workshops.

Share

I would love to hear your feedback, stories, and responses to this book. To contact the author, go to www.PoweredByMeNow.com or send an e-mail to sheri@PoweredByMeNow.com.

Introduction

Powered by Me®

When I first started writing this book, I wanted to contribute to positive change in education. However, the final stages of this process awakened me to a new intention. My purpose is to cultivate acceptance and to guide educators on viewing themselves from a higher mind as creators with unlimited potential. Acceptance in the now supports authentic movement from the depths of compassion. This stirs perception, permitting the revelation of self-imposed obstacles. It is neither necessary nor helpful to rehash some of the obstacles living and breathing among educators today, which include the suppression of creativity, instinct, and self-expression. I intend to focus on resources that free you from distracting perceptions, beliefs, outside influences, and short-term (quick-fix) strategies. Upping the educational ante on standards, expectations, and professionalism may very well be appropriate and necessary. However, in order to truly make a difference in the lives of students and their families, one must not negate the power of individual and group consciousness. In its absence, educators are susceptible to the tug of perfectionism, self-criticism, negativity, burning out, and frustration, all of which weaken the self, clogging pathways to higher teaching potential.

Tools and Strategies

Consider this book a toolbox of super potential, practices robust with effects well beyond the classroom. What makes them so powerful is *every* single strategy in this book is mutually beneficial, to you, your students, and others. Not only are you exposed to new ways of handling the classroom, but you also electrify the more familiar ones. This is not meant to replace or even add to your collection, as that would imply the ineffectiveness of your current practice. There lies the reason why I wrote this book. Although often unspoken, the idea of not being, doing, or working hard enough is capable of searing the roots of who you are. What is happening around you, opposed to inside, dictates your experiences. If your students are focused and performing well, you may feel peaceful, if they are struggling, you may also struggle. One of the intents of the strategies in this book is to soften the voices around you, the voices of policy makers, administrators, parents, colleagues, and students. As they soften, your voice and its ties to your inner body are pronounced, carving the way for presence and deeper experiences with yourself and others.

The tools and strategies you currently utilize with your students may not change. However, how, why, and when you use them may. Your awareness is what modifies a teaching tool coming *from* you to a tool that comes *through* you. Tools that come *through* you carry your potential, passion, purpose, vibration, and strength.

Throughout the book, I have included studies that support this way of being. Also included are **Try This!** practices and classroom examples you may relate to. They are opportunities to experience mindfulness. The **Try This!** practices are simple and, at times, purposely playful. To begin, I would highly suggest you read the entire book. If you skip ahead, you may dismiss the power of process. This book is more than knowledge, it is an experience. Your experience with the **Try This!** practices prepares you for incorporating mindfulness into the classroom. Some of the strategies are direct while others move through quiet observations of self. One is not better or more effective than another. Allow yourself time to truly absorb and play with the material. This book is less about doing and more about being.

Powered by Me®

You are a resource of unlimited potential, according to the Powered by Me® mindset. Who you are goes well beyond what you do. Your awareness of your beliefs, thoughts, attention, action, and effort shapes the experiences within you as well as outside of you. Your power is strengthened through practices that unify the mind, body, and breath. With guidance, consistency, and commitment, these practices set consciousness in motion. Higher consciousness is the part of you that contains the utmost respect for self. When thoughts, decisions, and responses are generated from this place, you become an unconditional source of support, inspiration, and connection.

Five Tenets of Powered by Me®

Powered by Me® is based on five beliefs:

1. To truly empower another individual, you must first empower yourself.

2. The power does not lie in the tools but rather in the individual using the tools.

3. True power comes from the gathering of many individuals with a likeminded intention.

4. People do better when they feel better.

5. Finally, *Powered by Me*® is a collective shift that focuses on what you, your school community has rather than what it lacks.

The publication of this book is timely as 2012 marks the eleventh anniversary of No Child Left Behind, a long journey of collecting data, identifying problems, and brainstorming solutions. In the mean-time, teacher retention rates in the United States have hit an all time low since the 1980s and "teacher attrition has grown by fifty percent over the past fifteen years" (Forbes.com, 2011). As educators and policy-makers continue to collect, sort through, and learn from the data, alternatives with compelling benefits are finding their place in it all.

As the movement of awareness pedals into schools across the world, its amazing attribute of connecting human beings of all backgrounds, ages, and abilities speaks volumes. Researchers such as Emiliana Simon-Thomas, a neuroscientist at Stanford University, report how compassion (generated from awareness) is a "natural instinct which has been observed by children as young as one years of age"(Simon-Thomas, 2012, p. 81). There are no limitations. The only form of resistance is within the individuals themselves. To truly support this inner movement, it must come through the educators themselves. This requires a conscious shift from teaching what you know to becoming the change you would like to see.

I hope you enjoy this book as much as I enjoyed the process of writing it. To those of you on the frontlines who are doing the work more directly, thank you. I leave these seeds with you, and may the breath of your awareness water them.

"Become the change you would like to see." *Gandhi*

CHAPTER 1

Manifesting Your Teaching

How you see yourself has a tremendous impact on how you teach your students. If you see yourself as free, then examples of freedom will unfold in front of you. These include taking risks, opening to new ways of learning, offering ideas, problem solving, working beyond expectations, respecting individual differences, working independently, sharing openly, and getting along better with others. Witnessing these reflections naturally alters your teaching. However, you cannot witness what you don't see. If you are free, you no longer need to cope or survive the experiences of your day. You become less encumbered by what you are working toward, what is expected of you, and what you are attempting to prevent. This is replaced by a growing interest in what is happening inside you in the exact moment. The present moment is your greatest treasure. The more energy you generate, the less likely you are to resist, or control what is happening around you. This energy is different from the energy you use to teach or complete tasks. It originates from inside and is expanded through focus and awareness. To begin this journey, you must see yourself as already free, and with that freedom springs honor, truth, effectiveness, and a deeper connection to your love of teaching.

Are You Repeating or Teaching?

The energy you choose to invest in is the energy that will most likely be repeated. If your thoughts are colored with deficiency the energy generated from those thoughts is likely to be repeated. For example, imagine thinking *I don't get paid enough for what I do.* This thought generates energy, which contributes to your belief system. If you think this thought over and over, you may start to believe that your worth is based on how much money you make. Accordingly, an administrator (who gets paid more money) is worth more than a teacher. This kind of belief system erodes self-esteem and contributes to the development of cultural myths.

Without awareness, the energy of your belief system may imitate itself at some point in your day. Could the disappointment of your paycheck be related to the disappointment you feel about a student's work? The power of the subconscious mind has been studied by psychologists and scientists extensively throughout history. In your mind, you are teaching. However, in your subconscious mind, you may *also* be reiterating your inner thoughts and beliefs. Chris Howard, author and co-founder of The Academy of Wealth and Achievement, states, "Perception is projection." This means how you handle situations in your day is highly connected to the experiences of your inner atmosphere.

The Process

The process of cultivating freedom lies within your own self-awareness. This book leads you through the process from the viewpoint of working in an educational setting. Trust the process. Trust that your interest in this book is enough. Allow the energy generated from your interest to lead the way. Along the way, you may encounter speed bumps. A speed bump is a feeling or sense that encourages you to pause while you are reading, perhaps to digest the material. Each speed bump is there for a reason. Try not to rush through them, as the speed bumps are linked to moving through potential roadblocks. Roadblocks are feelings that are held back or pushed away; speed bumps, however, are your *awareness* of the roadblocks. Moving through roadblocks is deeply powerful. Moving through your roadblocks in an educational community is transformational.

This chapter begins with recognizing possible roadblocks. Recognizing your roadblocks is essential for setting up the foundation you are about to embark upon (chapter 2). Please do not skip ahead. That is a prime example of leaping over a roadblock. By doing so, you may undermine the power of process.

ROADBLOCKS

Below I have identified possible roadblocks as power myths and power suckers. Power myths are beliefs and perceptions that are learned. Power suckers are actions, reactions, and habitual responses that may occur passively or actively. Passive responses typically take place in your head in the form of self-talk. Active responses are what you choose to do with those thoughts. Everyone has power myths or power sucker experiences. It does not matter where or why they exist. What matters is how they are maintained. When myths and suckers are left unspoken, and are never truly allowed to rise to a conscious level, you may feel held back or inhibited from being able to function from your highest potential.

As you review each myth, notice how you feel and if you can resonate in any way. Listen to yourself as you read each myth either out loud or silently. Notice your tone of voice, speed, and any thoughts that come up. Each myth is followed by an illustration of truth. The purpose is to show you how to see each myth in another way.

POWER MYTHS

Power Myth: I have no choice
Truth: You always have a choice.

Power Myth: Being in your power means you are very laid back and never get angry.
Truth: Being in your power means you are real. You have real feelings. However, your feelings do not define you, your values, competence, or your belief system.

Power Myth: Your students' progress reflects your power as a teacher.
Truth: Your true power is not based on outcome of others but in the way you chose to see the process.

Power Myth: There is only one way to teach and one way to learn.
Truth: Appreciating learning styles create capable students and teachers.

Power Myth: Assessments allow you to see where your students are weak and where you are failing.
Truth: Assessments serve as tools for knowledge, communication, and setting goals.

Power Myth: I know I am powerful if I am popular.
Truth: Teaching is not a popularity contest. Worth based on numbers is only an illusion of power. Feedback from others is simply an opinion.

Power Myth: You are what you do.
Truth: It is not about what you do but who you are.

Power Myth: When everyone is happy, then I can be happy.
Truth: Happiness is a feeling, becoming your own source of inspiration is a mindset.

Power Myth: If I had more time, I could do better.
Truth: Time is a roadblock that leads to the power sucker doubting one's abilities.

Power Myth: Power is the ability to survive all situations.
Truth: Power is the ability to move through all situations.

Try This!

Treat power myths as a community journal. Write down your myths and consider opening up a dialogue of myths amongst your colleagues. You may want to temporarily hang up a blank poster board with two columns in the teacher's room. On one side have individuals anonymously state their myths and on the other side have them state their truth. Writing myths and replacing them with truths loosens the grip they hold over you. Community journals are a way to share courage and wisdom. Individuals who may not be ready, or who are unable to truly see the undercurrent of myths, may witness them more easily through others.

POWER SUCKERS

Your greatest power sucker is when you think too much and your thoughts are predominately stressful. Thinking and stress are the catalyst of many power suckers, a few of which I have listed below. Being able to distinguish power sucker thoughts from thoughts that boost your awareness not only saves you time and energy, but offers you *more* time and energy. If you really stop and notice the amount of time devoted to thinking, re-thinking, or even dwelling on certain thoughts, it explains why you may feel squeezed for time. Recognizing power suckers is a way to cut the time you spend on them in half maybe more. Here is an example. Imagine you had to make a decision about whether to reschedule a field trip. Typically you may spend time being indecisive about the weather, student reactions, scheduling difficulties, parental complaints, transportation, etc. *Now*, knowing that over-thinking is a power sucker you may choose to reschedule the field trip, notify the people that need to know, and then move on. No dwelling, no second guessing just a clear response to what needs to be done at that moment. One of the greatest pieces of advice I ever received when I was struggling over whether to accept another job, was to make my decision and not look back. Second guessing steps over your inner voice causing you to hang on to the past. Watch for the moments when your mind drifts back or launches forward. This book shows you how training yourself to be in the moment offers you energy, peace, trust in yourself, and yes, time.

Below are illustrations of feelings and behaviors that may lead into power suckers: talking, gossip, and doubt. As you explore them you may notice how one power sucker breeds another. For example, stress breeds thinking and too much thinking may lead to gossip. I must confess, my first few drafts of power suckers were a fairly comprehensive list. It wasn't until I finished the last chapter that I realized I had sucked the process away from you. By giving you the answers (which are my opinions based on my personal experiences) I was removing you from the process of liberating yourself from myths and suckers. The examples below illustrate how suckers work in partnership with myths. As always feel free to add to this list on your own or amongst others. Included are **Try This!** practices that will help you with the liberation process.

Talking

Talking is one way to convey and teach information. However, speaking unconsciously may drain you of valuable energy, reinforcing the power myth: There is only one way to teach and one way to learn. Learning to transform your speech into conscious communication builds self-awareness, comprehension, and rapport with your students. When talking evolves into lecturing, over-explaining, or continuously repeating the same things, it is similar to having a slow leak in a tire. The tire still may work, however, over time it will become less reliable. Have you ever witnessed someone speaking to students who appear to be distracted or disinterested in what the teacher has to say? Unconscious speech is something that grows out of habit or in reaction to stress.

In Chapter Two you will revisit speech from a building block perspective. The purpose of this section is to show you how your uses of speech maybe a power sucker. Remember power suckers slowly suck you out of the present moment, disconnecting you from your mind, body, and spirit (roadblock). When this happens you may say things out of reactivity. Once in reactive mode your potential to read and respond to your students is spared at the expense of your own energy. Recognizing the difference between reactive speech and conscious speech is like lifting the shade on a window. It sheds light, allowing you to see situations and relationships with your students clearly while feeding you the benefits of consciousness.

The process of developing conscious speech includes a look at how talking may be draining you or diminishing your effectiveness. When it comes to personal development there is no end or limitation, everyone can benefit from a look at their own speech. Below are characteristics that clarify the difference between the two. As you read through them notice how conscious speech is more rooted in the present moment. Conscious speech allows you to have a deeper experience with yourself and others. It stems from having a solid foundation (chapter 2). Unconscious speech stems more from the notion of getting it done.

Unconscious Speech

» Speaking quickly or attempting to provide a lot of information in a short period of time.

» Rushing explanations, questions, or comments.

» Using the same tone, volume, or pitch of voice.

» Repeating the same words or explaining things the same way each time (e.g. always starting with, "Boys and girls…"

Conscious Speech

» As you speak you are aware of your body and breath. For example, you may notice your feet standing on the floor or the location of your breath in your chest.

» You are able to scan the room and read the body language, and facial expressions of your students (without judgment).

» You vary your voice tone. For example you may consciously lower your voice to encourage a calming atmosphere.

» You intentionally pause between words or sentences allowing a moment for the material to sink in, or an opportunity for questions and comments.

» Your directions are clear and concise.

» You ask open ended questions.

» You watch your assumptions or pay attention to the facts opposed to mind reading.

Try This!

Ask open ended questions. Open ended questions invite presence and connection into the process, often sparking insight and dialogue. They help you get to know who your students *are*.

If you had all the time you wanted what would you create?

How are you prepared for the next steps?

What is your plan?

Where are you in the process?

What strategies work best for you?

How did you prepare in your head for this assignment?

What are your thoughts?

How do you feel?

What do you notice about?

What do you think?

Tell me about your picture.

Tell me one thing I might not know about you.

What is your passion?

If you had a wish what would it be?

Gossip

Gossip works hand in hand with the myth I know I am powerful if I am popular. It is a learned behavior that may be reinforced through media, family, peers, and community. It is a way people compare themselves to others and cope with pressure.

If gossip is strong in the school environment it is a pretty good indication that anxiety levels are high. Gossip promotes perfection, paranoid behavior, tension and low self-esteem all of which easily lead to miscommunication. Conversely, less gossip indicates that people are paying more attention to how they connect to themselves and others. Partnership, creativity, and team work all thrive in environments based on connection.

Below is an outline of a four step process for working through the roadblocks of gossip. You can apply this process to any roadblock (myth or sucker). Notice how speed bumps are an opportunity for consciousness.

SPEED BUMPS

1. Speed bumps are your inner brake pedal. Think about the way you go over a speed bump. Typically, you take the time to slow down and feel the motion of the bump. Treat gossip the same way pause and feel the motion of gossip. Pay attention to how it impacts you inside. Does it elevate your heart rate, creating tension, or do you feel an electrical charge from it? Just notice. Now notice the motion outside of you. Notice the body language of others, colors in the room, shadows etc.

2. Listen to the gossip in your head. Are you comparing yourself or situations to each other? If you find yourself judging, state the word, *energy* to yourself and feel the motion of judgment. Keep it light. Talk out loud to your speed bumps. Say "thank you, speed bump, for bringing me back to the moment." If the word energy does not help you shift, Dr. Zoe Marae recommends calling it a word that discourages you from judging yourself such as: broccoli. She states, what you call it does not matter, you noticing your thoughts does.

3. Experience the energy of the roadblock (gossip). Experiencing the energy of a roadblock is like taking a shower. When you are in the shower you are most likely feeling the temperature of the water, water pressure, and sensations on your skin. This will make more sense to you once you read chapter two and three.

4. Notice when you apply the above steps the amount or frequency of gossip around you dissipates. Again this process may be applied to any roadblock.

Jane met with a regular lunch group for almost the entire year. The group met at the same time daily in the same classroom. Very often what seemed an innocent gathering turned into a circle of complaining and sarcasm. Individuals that walked by would often hear the group laughing and looking over their shoulders' to see if anyone was coming. Most individuals outside of the group ignored what was happening. However, the dynamics from the group seemed to contribute to an atmosphere of distrust and separation from others.

When Jane applied the four step process to her lunch gatherings she received much insight about herself, including the mistaking of gossip as connection. Through awareness of her inner brake pedal (speed bump) Jane was able to connect with others through what was happening *inside* of her rather than through gossip. This awareness allowed Jane to view her students in a new light. When gossip occurred in the classroom Jane no longer ignored it or lectured her students about it. Instead she chose to teach her students about the value of their own speed bumps.

Try This!

Teachers Room. Consider eating in environment where individuals are encouraged to be mindful of what they say. Be open to having conversations with individuals you may not typically interact with.

Pay attention to the time of day, location, and topics that generate gossip. Ask yourself, how can I maintain my integrity during those times? Author Amy Ahlers suggests you let people know you are doing a "gossip cleanse." She suggests replacing gossip with good talk, for example words of inspiration or positive statements. She also reminds people to include *all* gossip in this practice (even the gossip about celebrities).

DOUBT

When myths such as: If I had more time I could do better and I have no choice, permeate the atmosphere the shadows of stress and doubt surface. I choose doubt to focus on because it depletes the soul, meaning it disconnects you from connecting to your source of strength. The truth is, as you learn in Chapters Two and Chapter Three you always have a choice when it comes to your sensory system. You decide how and in what way you would like to focus your senses. Your students also have a choice. Your job is not only to present choices but to step out of the way once choices are made (unless of course the choice may cause harm). The example below illustrates the sucker of doubt. Notice how the prevention specialist chose to step out of the way rather than try to fix or make the teacher feel better. See how this led to greater insight on the teacher's part.

> *Prevention specialist, Cindy Horgan remembers volunteering in a classroom to support an activity Celebrating Fall. The teacher asked if Cindy would lead the project. Cindy chose to make an apple pie with the preschool class. The classroom watched while Cindy gathered the materials and directed the project. During the process Cindy could sense that her less structured teaching style put the teacher on edge. The teacher stood with her arms crossed, interacting with the students only when she thought they were misbehaving or not paying attention. The final product looked like a hodge podge quilt of crust.*
>
> *The teacher later confided in Cindy about her personal struggle with the process. Not only was it difficult to let go, but in that moment she found herself doubting her own abilities. Cindy's ability to move at ease reflected the teacher's own feelings of unease. Her initial reaction was to try to stop the unease (doubt) by controlling the behavior of her students.*

The situation above is not about what went wrong. It is more an illustration of what can grow from the sucker of doubt. The goal is not to eliminate power suckers but rather to get to know them by allowing them to play out with awareness. The process of developing your strength and awareness naturally dissolves suckers. Like development the process of working through suckers has no end. Suckers do not change. However with awareness *you* change. With practice and consciousness suckers lose their charge.

THE EMOTIONAL ROLLER COASTER

Without awareness power suckers take you on an unconscious emotional roller coaster ride. One minute you may feel confident, the next you feel a bit unsteady. You may also witness this emotional roller coaster ride in your students. History shows that many of us have learned to become accustomed to things worsening before they improve. Take the example of studying for a test. How many of us have learned that you have to get through the hard part studying before you can get to the rewarding good grades? This kind of teaching diminishes the power of process and trains you and your students to believe that relief and freedom come solely from outcome.

Smoothing out the roller coaster ride of emotions requires presence and a willingness to listen to your internal story. I have been reading self-help books and attending wellness seminars since I was a teenager. My mother was so fearful that events in my life would lead me to a dark place that she purchased every book in print as well as audio on learning how to love myself. The emotional roller coaster of ups and downs did not fully click until a recent experience.

> *I woke up one morning at four thirty a.m. and started thinking about my book. By 4:45 a.m. I was tip toeing out of bed to see if I could sneak in an hour of writing before my husband and children woke up. The days had been so filled with my children's activities that I had been struggling to find another way. Once I got in front of my computer the words weren't coming. I was tired and regretted my decision to get out of bed. By 6 a.m. the house was starting to wake up and I found myself standing in front of the refrigerator with the door open. That is when my stories (my imagination) started. In my mind I created the story of my day. There is no milk, and no eggs, guess I will be going to the grocery store today. That means no gym time for me and right now I feel so tired I probably*

*will have no writing time as well. Everyone else in this house seems
to have the freedom to take care of themselves except for me.*

My inner thoughts continued as I served breakfast fully expecting my family to be unappreciative of my cooking and prepared their lunches. They started to wonder, *what is wrong with mom.* Before I knew it unfriendly words were being exchanged between my husband and me. Later that morning when I was in the shower, a light bulb went off in my head. I had done exactly what I was writing about. I had learned that I need to suffer before things get better.

Throughout the day I closed my eyes and tried to imagine the world of a teacher. What kind of stories might go through a teacher's head? When I was a school psychologist, I remember working on a report in my office. Before I knew it a staff member would appear in my office looking for support. One of the stories I created in that moment was, *Guess I won't have time to finish that report today.* I thought of a receptionist I used to work with who would hang a sign on her desk stating, "I am working on payroll." Everyone knew not to bother her if they wanted to get paid.

Author Geneen Roth writes about this in her book *Lost and Found: One Woman's Story of Losing Her Money and Finding her Life.* In it she states, "One of our main (an usually unspoken) beliefs is that it is only through shame, judgment, and deprivation that we truly change."(p.101, 2011).

What I discovered that morning was that it is not so much what is happening in the moment that sends us on a ride but rather the stories that are created in our minds. I convinced myself that I was deprived of time for myself. Stories or self-talk that generalize moments or create black or white thinking keep you locked into the ride preventing you from ever really experiencing anything fully. Below are words or phrases you may hear in your own inner stories. Think of them as a ticket that gets you on the ride to the roller coaster. If you do not chose to take the ride, or if you would like to get off the ride all you have to do is pause (speedbump) and allow yourself to *feel* your feelings from beginning, middle, end, and beyond. Try not to put end points on your feelings. You may feel uncertain about this Chapter Three reinforces how this makes your teaching more flexible and dynamic. For now pay attention to your tickets (thoughts, stories, imagination). Below are some examples:

Tickets

I'll never.
I can't.
I better.
Everything.
Nothing.
I should.

TRY THIS!

Create a word wall of "Right now," I have." Or "Right now, I am." When I looked into my refrigerator all I saw was what I did not have. Imagine if everyone began (and ended) their day focusing on what they *do have* in the exact moment they are in. For example, I have: my breath, choices, warmth, a place to teach. Focusing on what you *have* alters your perception allowing you to see things as they truly *are*.

EVERYTHING BEGINS WITH THE BREATH

Your breath is your most valuable resource. Not only does it maintain the inner workings of your body, it connects you to your nervous system, your senses, insight, and energetic self. Essentially your breath is your direct connection to consciousness. Therefore, no two breaths are exactly the same. Each breath offers you insight into your thoughts, feeling, and sensations. It is capable of intensifying or cooling down emotions, or present situations. When your breath is applied to your teaching it transforms daily tasks, to do lists and classroom management into the sensitivities of inner guidance.

Most people were never truly taught how to breathe. The science of breath has been studied for thousands of years by mind / body practices such as yoga and tai chi. This section teaches the basics of breathing: as a way to relieve stress, create emotional stability, increase energy, and shift yourself from reactivity to responsiveness. Once you feel comfortable with the technique of breathing, incorporating it into your classroom becomes natural. Keep in mind the art of breathing well is a life-long journey. It is not to be confused with a quick fix. However, conscious breathing is proven to improve: mood, energy, memory, circulation, immune system, stress reduction, and pain management. The utilization of breath is a graceful way to open the hearts and minds of you and your students.

BREATHING BASICS

Below are basic guidelines for learning how to breathe well. In the beginning it may feel somewhat robotic. However, when practiced regularly it feels more normal. Begin by breathing consciously for one to two minutes a day. Gradually increase this to twice a day. Once you experience the benefits, you may find yourself incorporating conscious breathing throughout your day. Try not to put pressure on yourself to do it right or if you miss the practice allow yourself a fresh start. The fact that you noticed you were not consciously breathing *is* progress.

» Sit or stand up tall. In order to breathe efficiently it is important to have a long spine. If you are sitting be sure to have your ankles directly under your knees, keeping them about hip width apart. If you are standing, stand with your feet hip width apart. Be sure your feet are straight. Try to balance yourself evenly between the balls and heels of your feet.

» Press shoulders back and down. Loosen your shoulders by rolling them forward and backward. Imagine trying to touch your ear lobes with your shoulders. You may find this movement addresses any tightness in your neck. Feel free to roll your neck around (both directions) and slide your chin back so ears land over your shoulders. Keep your chin parallel to the floor. Now you are ready to gently press your shoulders back and down creating space in your chest and heart.

» Relax your jaw. Notice if your teeth are clenched or your lips are pierced. Allow your jaw to relax and your bottom lip to be full. You may need to open your mouth wide a couple of times to encourage your jaw to release. Separate your lips slightly. Your lips are still connected but not sealed.

» Set your gaze. Efficient breathing takes concentration and effort. If your eyes are shifting around the room, this distraction will be reflected in the quality of your breath. Find one point to look at (preferably something not moving) and lower your eye lids (not your neck) so you are gazing rather than staring. See if you can hold your attention for at least one breath cycle of one inhale and one exhale.

» Nostril breathing. Breathing in and out from your nose is more calming to your nervous system than breathing through your mouth. It balances your nervous system by taking in oxygen and expelling carbon dioxide. Notice how breathing with your mouth closed requires you to take fewer breaths, spending less energy.

» Feel. Pay attention to how and where your breath moves through your body. The expansion of your lungs, side waist, kidneys (lower back), diaphragm and belly. Think of your belly in three parts. The lower under the navel, the middle, just above the navel and the upper, just below your sternum. On inhale, your belly blows up like a balloon and on exhale it deflates by gently pulling navel to spine.

» Breath count. Consider counting your inhalations and exhalations beginning with the number one and ending up to the number five. Inhale 1,2,3 and Exhale 1,2,3, 4. Counting your breath may help you concentrate and gives you and your students a guide for what it feels like to inhale and exhale fully.

Jill is a preschool teacher for four year olds who admits feeling ashamed about passing on her more challenging students to the public kindergarten. During one of our consultations Jill revealed that she felt her student's behaviors were a reflection of her teaching abilities. She silently worried what other teachers would think or say about her.

Jill is a teacher I consulted with to teach her calming techniques. Before learning how to breathe Jill felt angry and resentful toward the administration. She felt overworked, underpaid, and underappreciated for her work. I began the consultation with teaching her as well as the other staff members the basics of breathing. After three sessions Jill's breath brought her feelings of shame to a conscious level. Through some coaching and open conversation she was able to move through her shame. This movement allowed her to feel better about herself and her job. Jill also reported the benefits of breathing extending into her home life.

How Breathing Affects Mood and Attitude

Your breath has the ability to elevate your mood and alter your attitude as it is directly tied to your nervous system. When your breath is shallow or rapid it stimulates your sympathetic nervous system which is responsible for fight or flight. Fight or flight mode triggers your body in the following ways: increased heart rate, hardening of the abdomen, elevated blood pressure, constricted blood vessels, slower circulation, dilated pupils, body temperature shifts and increased cortisol levels (stress hormones). These triggers are often experienced as anxiety, nervousness, stress, and tension. On the other hand, when your breath is slower or fuller it taps into your parasympathetic nervous system. This system slows your heart rate down, lowers blood pressure, improves circulation, relaxes your muscles, and broadens perception. Stimulating your parasympathetic nervous system allows you to respond to situations more mindfully. Your ability to listen and connect to others increases, and you may find yourself flowing from one thing to the next with more ease. As your perception widens you become less judgmental or critical of yourself and others. The more you practice the art of breathing the less energy you waste, meaning you actually take fewer breaths throughout the day.

Studies on blood analysis illustrate this further. Cells that receive more oxygen actually function and appear healthier. Doctors such as Marcelle Pick, who is the co-founder of Women to Women Clinic in Yarmouth, Maine and (Author of *Are You Tired and Wired?*) are using blood analysis to determine whether a patient is taking in enough oxygen or expelling enough carbon dioxide. Marcelle states, "When you are not inhaling enough oxygen or exhaling enough carbon dioxide the consequence may be fatigue, mental fog, and decreased tissue function." She often recommends to her patients, "Learn how to breathe" (April 20, 2011). When your cells are not functioning efficiently this not only influences their ability to transport essential nutrients (e.g. glucose, and feel good hormones, oxygen) but also inhibits your body's ability to remove toxic waste (e.g. carbon dioxide, stress). All of which have a significant impact on mood. The bottom line is breathing makes you and your students feel better and is a natural resource for enhancing mood.

THE THREE AGREEMENTS

Roughly ten years ago I read a book called *The Four Agreements*, by Don Miguel Ruiz (1997). One evening I sat at the edge of my bed staring at my bookshelf while reflecting on the conclusion of Chapter One. The book, *The Four Agreements* practically jumped off my book shelf, dust and all. Revisiting this book not only reminded me of how the process of self-awareness is non-linear but also how embarking on the road of self-awareness is a way to honor the agreements of your soul. No matter what your beliefs are religious, non-religious, or spiritual, you are on the path of educating and supporting others for a reason. Consider the agreements below to be your pledge. Pledges are ways to remind ourselves of where we come from, and what we stand for.

The purpose of the specific agreements written below is preparation for the guide foundation (chapter 2). Consider these agreements a pledge with your higher self. Your higher self is the part of you that holds yourself in the highest regard. It is what you feel in your heart. The part of you that see's yourself as a creator and contributor to the world around you.

Agreement One: *All* of my feelings are a resource for strength.

Agreement Two: I am already enough and therefore my students are already enough.

Agreement Three: My awareness is powerful.

Agreement One: All of my feelings are a resource for strength.

If you are breathing, you are feeling. By making this agreement you are choosing to experience anything you have been accustomed to suppressing, denying or covering up as a means for coping with a position that requires stamina, stability, and strength. Seeing your feelings as a source of strength gives you permission to experience them. As you will see in Chapter Three, your feelings supply you with energy, focus, and presence. To deny your feelings is similar to denying your inner strength.

For some the process of experiencing feelings may appear challenging. Please do not allow it to deter you from making this agreement. This agreement offers you something to focus on. If you see your feelings as a source for strength, you will naturally start to attract and recognize moments that allow you to encounter them. For some this may be an introduction to the process. For others it is a way to deepen it.

To help you accept this agreement there are two rules of thumbs to consider:

1. Experiencing your feelings is a bodily experience, not a mental one. For example, if you yawn you may feel tears in the corners of your eyes. You may feel your muscles relax or the tension in your chest begin to loosen up. Yawning then becomes a way to experience your feelings.

2. You do not always have to label or know the feeling you are experiencing to release it. Thinking about what you are feeling is a way to maintain thinking which may prevent you from feeling. Chapters Two and Three explain this further.

TRY THIS!

Close your eyes and notice the energy around your throat. Notice how the air flows in and out of your throat. Pay close attention to the flow of air swirling around, massaging the back of your throat. Notice if you have a desire to cough, yawn, or clear your throat. Think of all the times you hold back your cough, yawn, sigh, or urge to clear your throat. This is the beginning of you noticing how your body naturally wants to create space for the experience of feeling.

Agreement Two: I am already enough and therefore my students are enough.

This agreement frees you from the need to fix or change your students. When you see yourself as enough, you will then begin to see that your students are already enough. Seeing your students in this way shifts your role from finding what is wrong to providing feedback about what is right. The strategies or techniques you utilize with your students may not change. What changes with this agreement is your ability to surrender. As a teacher all you can do is your best with the knowledge and experience you have in that moment. Once you have given it your best effort and full attention, it is important to allow yourself to succumb to this agreement. Relinquish the need to rescue or control what may not be in your control. This preserves your energy and keeps you from becoming distracted from your true purpose.

I remember watching my daughter in a group situation. The group was receiving awards from their teachers. I listened and watched the process of handing them out. My daughter did not receive one. Later I spoke to her about this experience.

> *There will be many times in your life when you will watch other people get recognized for what they do. As you watch other people receive awards I would like you to focus on these words, I am already enough. Be happy for those individuals. Celebrate with them. Believe that you already have what you need. Your happiness for them is a way to show happiness for who you are.*

TRY THIS!

You are already enough. Many people fear that telling their students or children they are already enough will prevent them from striving. The words, you are already enough, mean that you were born with the resources and abilities that allow you to reach your highest potential. Once you read Chapter Two this will make more sense.

Agreement Three: My awareness is powerful.

You have the ability to expand anything you pay attention to. Your awareness stimulates volume, intensity, rate and depth. Focusing on something or someone in the *same* way over and over creates habitual patterns. Think of your focus as similar to the ocean tide. The tide changes direction every six hours, creating a cyclical pattern varying in volume, intensity, and rate. Your cyclical patterns are your sequence of neuro activity. Your perception may be a reflection of a these patterns. With awareness you have the ability to shape them in a way that benefits you and your students.

Consider your thoughts about a students work habits. If you see the student as always distracted or disruptive, question whether your viewpoint is being grooved by the makeup of your neuro activity, influencing your perception. If you continue to focus on the student's disruptiveness this increases the likelihood that you will associate distractibility with this student. Overtime you may develop a pattern of seeing the student in this way. Your view of this student may become ingrained in your memory and continue to be the way you think of this student long after he is in your class (in some cases years after).

Therefore, how you viewed this behavior grew in volume as you saw the distractibility at many different times during the day, rate as your thoughts about the distractibility were closer together, intensity you found yourself reacting or speaking to the student more often, and depth, as you began to experience tension in your body. You may not be able to measure whether the behavior grew in the student. However, your own awareness gives you information on how the student's behavior grew in you.

Science is now recognizing the power of focus. People have been utilizing the power of focus in many ways for thousands of years whether it is through prayer, meditation, intention, goal setting, study, observation, teaching etc. By making this agreement you are acknowledging your focus as a resource for developing awareness.

Try This!

Gather, Store, Distribute. This technique was taught to me by author and master yogi Sarah Powers. Since the belly is one of the areas of the body that holds stress it is also an area that relieves stress. Begin by sitting or lying down. Be sure you are relaxed. As you take a long inhalation imagine yourself gathering your breath. On exhale begin to pool or store your breath into the abdominal region (three inches below the navel). Rather than pushing the breath out, direct the breath down to this region storing its benefits. Once stored allow the breath to expand and distribute itself into other parts of your body sending its vital nutrients.

CHAPTER 2

Expanding into the Guide Role

WHAT IS A GUIDE?

A GUIDE IS ANYONE WHO INTENDS to empower others through their own self-awareness. This book focuses on guides in the world of education, including teachers, support staff, administrators, and caregivers. A guide cultivates self-awareness by training himself to pay attention to what is happening inside as well as outside of his body. The consistency, commitment, and repetition of focused attention both inside and out endorse the creative engagement between teaching and becoming. The strength of this union allows educators to witness themselves from a place of power. Your place of power is your authentic self.

As a guide, the study of self-awareness helps you lead and inspire others well. This study includes: self-observation, knowledge, and daily encounters. Your experiences are your personal treasure chest. They are rich with insight about how you are responding to your work as an educator. Every response whether positive, negative, intense, or subtle aids the ripening of your unquestionable power; which arrives through the linking of you to your utmost self. In your utmost self, emotions are experienced rather than pushed aside or projected. You rather than your environment become the conductor of emotional flow. This emotional flow seams you to your work through focus, balance, internal motivation, and confidence. This balance is not measured in words or outcome. It is an immersion into the roots of who you are implementing a shift from teaching to guiding.

By the end of this chapter, you will be able to identify what a guide is, create a guide vision, understand the necessary ingredients for a guide foundation, honor your guide makeup, and identify any patterns that move you away from the guide direction. By following this process you are laying the groundwork for building on the guide role and teaching from your position of power.

Self-awareness is a unique blend of your experiences brought to your awareness through sensations in the body. Your experiences are your perceptions, thoughts, feelings, interactions, and reactions. You develop self-awareness by feeling and listening to your body. Each time you have a thought based on your perceptions it translates to the body in the form of sensation. Dr. Candace B. Pert author of *Molecules of Emotion* refers to this "massive information exchange occurring in the body as body music." She states: "the sum of the sounds of this body music is called emotions."If you sit up tall and take a very deep breath inhaling and exhaling, you will find behind the breath a trail of sensation. You can recognize it through tingly skin and gentle pulsing, both of which are a sign of inner movement. This is your music. The movement of your breath sets the tone for the characteristics of your music: loud, soft, calming, stimulating, steady, or silent. Your students may not be able to hear your music, but they can sense it. They sense it through their own sensitivity. However, depending on where they are developmentally and what they have learned about their emotions, they may attempt to control (stop) the experience of their own bodily wisdom. This is a mistaken way they learn to manage what feels uncomfortable. As a result, unconscious behaviors such as distraction, complaining, blaming, and ignoring, may occur. As their guide, you may not be exposed to these behaviors if the student chooses to bury them during school hours to release them later, if at all. The topic of behaviors is explored more fully in Chapter Five.

For some, the idea of being in the moment, as opposed to controlling what is happening in the moment, is a scary thought. However, most individuals fluctuate in and out of the present moment all day long. Not only is that normal, but healthy. The term guide is meant to be a tool of awareness, not a label or title. Unlike a report card that measures how you are performing the term guide is used as a means for checking in with yourself. Anytime you are present in the moment you are guiding. By being present you are working from your fullest potential. Your experiences are a culmination of your perceptions, sensations, feelings, thoughts, and beliefs. It is through a state of presence that you are truly able to meet the needs of yourself as well as your students. This process is not about changing who you or others are, but rather meeting yourself where you are at today.

Consider reflecting on teachers and educators who made a positive impact on you as a student. As you dig through these memories, notice if you revisit old feelings or sensations from the past. For example, in ninth grade, my English teacher, Mr. Weaver assigned all of his students a nick name. Not only was it impressive that he could remember all of the nicknames, but it was his tone of voice that still rings in my memory. To me he would say, "Good morning, Z" (which was the first letter of my maiden name). It felt as if in that brief moment he was not thinking about anything else. Twenty-six years later the memory still warms my heart and I continue to be lifted by the experience. As a teacher and guide, you impress students lives both academically and emotionally with long-term effective life memories. When teachers share stories, offer opportunities for success, share kind words, laugh, and play with their students they are creating memories. Memories are stored in both your brain and body. They are implanted into cellular memory through pictures and sounds. One of my daughter's teachers made a DVD of photos taken throughout the year, incorporating music to each theme. My daughter guards this DVD, referring to it as her best year yet.

To guide means to develop your inner teacher so you can assist others in developing theirs. It is not about being on your game one hundred percent of the time. It is a process of defining, creating, and delving into your inner resources.

Sherianna Boyle

Creating a Guide Vision

Being a guide requires inspiration and tenacity. One way to stay on track is to create a guide vision, a written document of your hopes and dreams as an educator. Your personal hopes and dreams serve as a tremendous source for inspiration. They represent what you care about, your values, beliefs, and your purpose.

Your guide vision is similar to building a personal mission statement. A mission statement provides direction, focus, clarity, and unity. Most likely your individual school or district has developed a school-wide mission statement. Without a mission statement, people can feel lost, disconnected, uncertain and unmotivated. By creating your own mission statement in addition to your schools, you maintain your I voice: I need, I will, I can, I am, I hope. Your I voice keeps you connected to your truth and helps you to distinguish which feelings are yours and which ones belong to others.

> *One year, a male student was accused of sexual harassment. I was supporting the families of both the alleged female victim and the perpetrator as they navigated through a highly emotional experience. In addition, I was hearing strongly from the school's administration, which was consulting with the district lawyer. Needless to say it was a stressful time for all involved. The boy's family was calling me daily and his mom would vent to me about the school. One day his mom called and I told her I could not speak with her. I requested she stop yelling at me. She was so angry about what looked to her as betrayal that she began to bully me at meetings. She would speak about what I was not doing and how unavailable I was. I dreaded the numerous meetings I had to attend to deal with this issue. Eventually, I withdrew because too much attention was being placed on me. Not only was I no longer being effective, I had lost my I voice.*

The policies and mission statements of the school district were not written specifically for me, they were written for the district at large. The stress had me questioning whether my position as a school psychologist was the right job for me. Had I had my own mission statement (guide vision) I could have used this tool as a way to refocus and connect to my inner

26

intentions. My effort to stay neutral and serve as a sounding board, in the moment seemed appropriate. However, I soon discovered this response inhabited shaky ground. The guide foundation, which you will soon learn about, anchors decision making through self-awareness. The art of listening, one of the building blocks in the foundation, includes the ability to listen to yourself. Had I noticed that I was practically holding my breath every time I got on the phone with this mom and having thoughts such as how am I going to get off this phone, I could have prevented a relationship from being built on venting. I contributed to a perception that venting equaled caring. A guide vision like the one below would have been helpful:

> *I am taking care of myself in addition to supporting others. My own self-care supports me in the guide role. I am taking time to listen to my body and breath. My body guides me to set healthy boundaries. I say no when I need to and I allow others to work out their differences directly. I am asking for help when needed. To help solidify this vision I could create a picture in my head of what taking care of myself looks like.*

In the Responsive Classroom program, a research-backed approach to supporting the whole child in elementary education, teachers learn how to set the tone for an entire year by asking their students what their hopes and dreams are. The program emphasizes how students are more likely to follow what they had a part in creating. Hopes and dreams are generated in the beginning of the year as a way to set a healthy foundation for learning. Your guide vision is a tool for transitioning *you* back into the school year. It is your source of inspiration, a way to maintain the guide role. By writing a guide vision at the beginning of each year, you re-ignite the power behind your vision. Using your I voice creates a vision as if it is already occurring. For example, instead of writing I will, state, I am. Speak from your guide role rather than to it. Keep it positive, simple and realistic. Ask yourself, in this moment what do I value, what is important to me, what excites me, what is my purpose and finally what can I receive? Include lessons you have learned about the past, such as the importance of healthy boundaries, taking time for yourself, asking and accepting help. By rewriting your guide vision each year you are honoring the lessons you have learned along the way. You are never the same teacher you were the year before.

Your guide vision is your personal mission statement keeping you tuned into your personal power. When you feel tired, distracted, or fearful, your guide vision lifts you up offering you a way to rebalance your system. Unlike your school's mission statement, your vision is recreated each year or more as necessary. As you study yourself and attain your goals, your vision is adjusted to meet your present intentions. Your guide vision does not need to be perfect. Pick up your pencil, take a deep breath, tune into your I voice, and on exhale begin to write. Even if it sounds unrealistic, write it down. Once it is written consolidate it into two or three sentences.

HONOR YOUR GUIDE MAKE-UP

Your guide make up makes you the individual you are. This includes your physical DNA, life experiences, lessons, family, culture, feelings, thoughts, beliefs, and more. My children will often ask me if I love them more than their siblings. My answer is always the same. I love you for your uniqueness. The more you value your own uniqueness the less likely you are to use comparisons as a way to measure your own self worth, a true power sucker.

Educators arrive at their positions with a backpack full of stories. There are stories of accomplishment, reconciliation, love, hardship, pain, loss, rejection, forgiveness, and more. The stories, containing shame, humiliation, or embarrassment can be the most difficult to come to grips with. As an individual as well as a professional revealing yourself to others in a constructive way requires a bit of grace. Grace includes a filter to decipher insight from pain. When information is shared from pain it is a way to communicate your woes. Sharing from your woes says, I never have time for myself, while sharing from insight says, I find if I leave fifteen minutes early I am more likely to take a walk. Certainly, the choice to share parts of yourself with others is your free will. Even if you decide to keep your personal life private you cannot hide from the memory and response of your own body. Anything buried eventually surfaces as unresolved emotion or experiences. Without your conscious awareness these burials may expose themselves through tension, headaches, stress, back pain, lack of zest for life, high blood pressure, reactivity, anxiety, and more. Matching feelings with experiences or placing meaning on each bodily symptom may be counterproductive.

Below is one of the many stories I carried in my backpack. I hid it well most especially I hid it from myself. By doing so, I inhibited my higher consciousness through the harboring of shame.

> *When I was eight years old a close family member got into a car accident and hit a tree. As a result, two young people died and two others were badly injured. A number of equally traumatic events followed. As a result our family decided to relocate in attempt to get away from the pain. It was not until I learned the skills of self-awareness that my pain was set free. However, these experiences have developed in me a deep compassion and empathetic ear for children and families who are suffering. These same emotions charged me to co-write a parenting curriculum, create a peer mediation program, conduct self-esteem groups for girls and write this book.*

Behind every educator there are most likely stories that have steered them to teaching. Perhaps they were bullied, struggled with learning, or grew up with a love of books. You bring honor to your guide makeup, when you embrace all parts of yourself. Some of the greatest leaders in history have amazing stories to tell. They were not born great leaders they became great leaders. Each has a plethora of stories explaining how they came to be, what they overcame, lived through, believed, and worked passionately toward.

Your guide make-up, is a unique blend of all that you are. It includes experiences that were in your control as well as others that were not. Give yourself permission to feel and finish any feelings from your guide history. Feeling is not the same as processing. To feel is to gain awareness or experience. Similar to a story feelings have a beginning, middle, and end. When a feeling is left unfinished it is similar to an unfinished project. You may have reminders of the project being unfinished. These feelings and reminders draw energy away from you causing you to feel a lack of focus or frustration. By completing the feelings of your past you begin to embody these experiences as sources of wisdom and strength. To finish means to allow sensations to move through you in the present moment. As you do this, the completion of these feelings past or present translate to energy and strength.

In a comfortable, quiet place, close your eyes, and take some deep breaths. Give yourself a few moments to relax. Relax, your jaw, shoulders, and facial muscles. Once you feel relaxed, ask your body to make you consciously aware of any previous feelings that need to be completed. What is the first thought or feeling that comes to mind? Consider holding your attention on it. Notice any sensations that come up with that feeling. Notice what you see, taste, and hear around you. Sit in these sensations, focusing your attention on them and allow them to surround you like a warm bath. After a few minutes open your eyes softly and continue to sit quietly. You can take it one step further by writing in a journal or drawing your feelings. Consider playing soft, soothing music to provide comfort. As always, if this feels overwhelming, do not hesitate to get professional help. A mental health professional, certified energy worker, or personal coach, can make all the difference in the world in just a few sessions.

Educators are human beings with real stories. Be proud of who you are and where you come from. You have been given the opportunity to influence others for a reason. Your guide makeup is about recognizing your life as a whole. By choosing to invite the sensations of your guide makeup to a conscious level you are able to share who you are with dignity and grace. This speaks volumes to your students as you empower them through knowledge of who you are and how you were directed to teaching.

THE GUIDE FOUNDATION

The guide foundation includes your tools for bringing self-awareness into action. These tools have been with you since you were born. They are your ability to communicate, including: speech, vision, listening, smell, touch, and taste. Most of us learned in kindergarten the basics of the five senses. Unfortunately, many were left to figure out the power of these senses on our own. The awareness of your basic senses, joined with intention and tools for healthy communication shape a steady guide foundation.

Communication

Communication is the foundation of all we do. The effectiveness or ineffectiveness of any relationship whether it be partner to partner, parent to child or teacher to student is based on healthy communication. The word communication immediately conjures the way you speak to others but really the foundation for communication encompasses the skills of listening, attention, touch, body language, intention, a connection to purpose and even your olfactory system. No one can give you a foundation; it is self-constructed through the guidance of people and experiences of the world around you.

Listening

Listening is more than just being quiet while another person speaks, it is our body language, our ability to reflect back to what has been said, the timing of our communication and we respond to our own bodily cues. It requires watching yourself for habitual responses or urges to fix the person in front of you. The art of listening is formed by two parts: first, learning how to listen to yourself and second, learning how to listen to others.

In *Light on Life* by B.K.S Iyengar, ears are referred to as "the window to the soul." Your emotions are the inner language connected to the self. The process of listening to yourself includes getting to know your emotions, how you label them, your attitude toward them, ways they are covered and how they show up. The book, *The Language of Emotions* by Karla McLaren states: "Our emotions convey messages between our unconscious and conscious minds and they give us the skills and abilities we need to deal with each situation we encounter." Your emotions are delivered to you in the form of sensations. However, if you are distracted by your thoughts, mental pictures or lists of things to do these sensations may seem unavailable or even non-existent in you. If you are busy analyzing which sensations belong to which feelings this may prolong feelings of discontent or anxiety. Keep in mind your idea of stress may be different from someone else's. Pay attention to what may be influencing your perceptions. Much of what you believe or rehearse is learned. Teachers, caregivers, parents, siblings, peers, media, and more influence the development of emotional habits (how you interpret and view your feelings).

One afternoon as I was walking into the library I saw a young boy and his caregiver in the parking lot, the boy was crying. I could hear the caregiver say over and over "You need to stop crying, no books until you stop crying." The four year old boy was sucking in his sobs, trying so hard to make it stop. He would stop and then soon start up again clearly frustrated by his inability to completely stop his emotions from flowing. These kinds of messages teach children at a very young age that it is not okay to feel your feelings. In fact, they are viewed as a weakness or interruption rather than an opportunity to listen from within. Had the boy been able to feel his sadness and finish his crying, he would have learned how to experience an emotion and move through it. Instead, he learned how to push it away.

The guide role allows you to rebirth your attitude toward your emotions. It provides an opportunity to transition from labeling them to describing them. A label has an undertone of permanency, which can lead to the belief that you are as good as the emotion you are experiencing. By tuning into your sensations you are more likely to experience the entire feeling rather than a portion, the beginning, middle, and end. For example, author McLaren, describes "sadness in its mood state slows us down and makes us stop pretending that everything is all right." By noticing the slowing down you are listening to the sadness. Rather than react to the sadness you can then respect it by resting, eating in silence, driving more slowly to work, and giving yourself breaks.

Now consider the emotion fear. How would you describe sensations associated with fear? Perhaps by an increased heart rate, wide eyes, nervousness, and repetitive thinking. One benefit of fear is that your mental alertness heightens your ability to work quickly. By noticing the quick bodily movements you are listening to your fear. It is through listening that feelings are allowed to surface to a conscious level where they can be more easily moved.

The more you are present with your feelings the easier it will be to hear them. This requires an honest look at how and when you shield them. Shields are both internal and external distractions from the present moment. Internal distractions include: consumption of thoughts, over focusing on other people's problems, things to do, events of the past, and places to be. External distractions are texting, side talk, T.V., computer, shopping, drinking, smoking etc. The more you consider what your feelings have to offer the less likely you will want to shelter them.

An attitude of appreciation and comfort naturally follows as you shift from labeling to describing an emotion. It is through describing your emotions that their inherit value is revealed. For example, *My belly feels tight and my legs feel restless.* However, labeling the feeling as anxious, or stressed leads to developing self-defeating stories or supporting the inner critic.

The second part of becoming an effective listener is practicing how to listen to others. Eighty percent of what people hear is portrayed through body language. How well you attend the conversation greatly influences how well it is received. If you are nodding in agreement while your eyes are shifting around the room the person you are communicating with will be more likely to hear your non-verbal body language. The non-verbal body language will communicate something such as, *I hear you but I am not really listening.* Your messages are more likely to get across when they are in alignment with your body language, when the verbal and the non-verbal are in sync. This is true even if it means stating in that moment that you are unable to listen and would like to speak at a later time. You are better off postponing a conversation than you are faking your way through it.

> *During Cindy's first year of teaching a new student entered the classroom. His mother had brought him to school and showed him all the fun he would have. With the support of a teacher he became involved in an activity. The mother, experiencing some distress with the process of saying goodbye, decided to sneak out when her son was not looking. It only took about two minutes for the little boy to realize what had happened. He was not happy. He became very upset as he searched for his mother and began to run towards the door to follow her. The other teachers tried to comfort him by unsuccessfully engaging him in another activity. The teachers continued to reassure him that he was going to be fine and he would see his mother after lunch. This was not making it any easier. As his distress escalated he ran down a long hallway to the exit. Cindy ran down the hall after him where she captured him at a dead end.*

With no place to go and Cindy a stranger to him he retreated by leaning up against the wall and sitting on the floor crying. Cindy sat down across from him as he cried. After a few moments the boy looked up with his head in his hand and said, "It's not fair, I love her so much." Cindy looked at him and responded, "It's not fair." At that moment he stopped, he had been heard. In his next breath he asked "If she had a phone at this place" so he could call his mom. That experience taught Cindy the power of listening.

The above example shows how making eye-contact and being at the physical level of the student turned the situation around. It illustrates how speaking to students and staff privately, offering few of your own words and repeating back what you hear them saying is a tool of awareness. In effective listening, our job is never to fix or change but rather to gain rapport through mirroring back what the person is saying.

The process of listening is twofold. It begins with learning how to listen to yourself. This includes describing your inner feelings, noticing how your feelings benefit you, recognizing ways you may be covering them up and using honor to foster appreciation for what you feel. The more you practice listening to yourself, the easier it becomes to listen to others. This partnership between listening from within and listening to others is the art of constructive listening.

INTENTION

One of the pillars of the guide foundation is setting intention. Intention is the choice to connect to your presence, purpose, and faith. Intentions differ from goals in that they "flow from and are created in the heart while goals are created in the mind," states life coach Kelly Lin. "Goals help you with direction and taking action while intentions support your integrity." A goal may be to complete a task, while an intention connects you to the task. Goals speak to the future and intention speaks to the present moment. Goals speak from the mind, while intentions speak from the heart.

You can set intention by taking a deep breath, closing your eyes, and tuning into your heart. You know you are coming from your heart when you hear yourself describing you in the moment: I care, I am, I see, I love, I feel, I can or May I. If you find yourself thinking about the future you have moved into thinking mode. Heart feels, while brain thinks. Whenever you consciously choose to be in the moment you are in the process of setting intention. Author Mazza Hillier states: "Intention is powered by faith." Faith in this case is the belief that your intentions are influenced by forces that extend beyond you. Faith knows that when you align your beliefs and thoughts with awareness you receive an opportunity to create intention. Your choices, purpose, and presence inflame the process. Purpose comes in all shapes and sizes. It can be as obvious as giving birth to a child or as obscure as giving someone a hug. The example below illustrates one scenario focused on setting a goal followed by a second example of adding intention.

> *Imagine you have been asked to meet some fellow teachers for lunch to discuss curriculum planning for the next several weeks. You prepare for the meeting by gathering your materials. The meeting takes place in a classroom just a few doors down. You arrive a few minutes early so the meeting can begin on time. As you sit in the room, you listen to the teachers discuss the curriculum from the previous meeting. Rather than discussing current goals, the group focused on what went wrong with the previous meeting. You feel irritated as you watch the time allotted disappear. The amount of time spent on rehashing the previous meeting left little time for planning. You leave the meeting feeling irritated that your time was wasted. This feeling increases throughout the day as you watch piles of work accumulating on your desk. You regret attending the meeting. If you hadn't wasted your time attending the meeting, perhaps you would have achieved some curriculum planning.*

Now, using the above example, once again you have been asked to join a group of teachers for lunch with the goal of planning curriculum. The goal has been pre-determined so you initiate the process of setting your own intentions. You do this by gathering your curriculum materials. Once your materials are gathered you pause, sit in your chair, close your eyes and take one deep breath (long inhale, long exhale). The first breath is to tune into your sensations. You open your eyes (softly) and take a second deep breath; this breath tunes you into your heart. Finally, you take a third complete breath (long inhale, long exhale) to set the intention. You make the intention: to prepare internally first before redirecting the group. *You will do this by joining your agitation in the moment by taking a long inhale through your finger tips and exhaling into your belly. If the group continues to stay off task you are now prepared to verbally redirect them.* Your intention becomes your tool as well as your anchor for respecting your own needs as well as the needs of others.

Setting goals without intention creates an imbalance between present and future. Through self-initiation of intention setting, you create balance between being and doing. This balance allows you to perform your job well while meeting your own needs.

The Power Of Touch

Studies have indicated a significant correlation between changes in how people think and feel after receiving a supportive touch. One study written in the New York Times revealed that students who received from a teacher a supportive touch on the back of the arm were twice as likely to volunteer in class as those who did not, (Feb 23, 2010, New York Edition, New York Times, pg. D5, *Evidence That Little Touches Do Mean So Much*). Healthy touch is a form of communication. Larry Ferlazzo a ESL, ELL, EFL teacher blogs on the power of light touch in the classroom. On April 18,[th] 2011, he posted a study that found "light touch on the upper arm can increase compliance substantially and two light touches can increase it even more."Touch can result in a higher positive response rate to a request for help", Larry Ferlazzo. (www.larryferlazzo.edublogs.org). Touch is one of your most valuable tools for communication and self-expression. Teachers can also receive the benefits by putting pressure onto their own skin. Through the form of self-massage you can increase the level of oxytocin in the body a chemical responsible for relieving stress, bonding, and building trust. "A warm touch reduces levels of the stress hormone cortisol."(Feb 23, 2010, New York Edition, New York Times, pg. D5, *Evidence That Little Touches Do Mean So Much*).

The Power of Sight (eyes)

How you visually scan a room directly impacts your nervous system. Your eyes receive information through the optic nerve allowing you to read and scan your environment. They have the ability to pick up on signals preparing you for alertness. Teachers are well versed at scanning the room checking to see if students need support and are on task. Notice however, if you have a habit of scanning in search of a problem. B.K.S. Iyengar said, "the eyes are the window to the brain." (*Light on Life*, 2005). The eyes reflect the way you see the world. Once you learn about the power behind your gaze, your eye-contact becomes an additional resource for restoring inner balance. Anything that impacts you on the inside, impacts your world on the outside. Your inner peace offers you the potential to tone down any behavior that shows up in front of you. If your eyes are wide and bulging you not only communicate anxiety, but are susceptible to picking up and intensifying the anxiety of those around you. Think of your eyes as an antennae picking up signals. Author and clinical psychologist Bo Forbes brought this concept to my attention at a workshop for anxiety and depression.(Kripalu Center, Lenox, MA.2007). To understand how this works I would suggest playing around with it. I know for myself that if my eyes are wide and scanning the room, my children pick up on my tension immediately. They might say: "What is wrong with mom?" or start to boss each other around in attempt to stop the discomfort they are picking up on. Your eyes do more than gain attention and build rapport with your students. They are one of the gateways to your inner world. Use your eyes to tone down a heightened state of arousal over time. You may see how this helps you expand your view of situations and individuals around you. The example below illustrates this further:

> *Imagine before going to school you have an argument with your spouse or one of your children. In the midst of the disagreement you look at the clock and realize that if you don't get going you may be late for work. Frazzled, you dash off to work. Your eyes are wide a look of panic on your face. You clutch the steering wheel as you drive. As you walk in the classroom, the children greet you with smiles and small talk. You suddenly realize that in order to do your job well, you need to calm down. You immediately tune into your eyes. They are wide and bulging. Through listening to your eyes you respond by turning off the fluorescent lights and telling the children they can read quietly for five minutes. As the children*

read, you sit in your chair and lower your gaze to your desk while taking long, slow breaths. Perhaps you have a picture on your desk of something soothing, a photograph of a flower or a place you find comforting. If you are gazing at a picture of a flower imagine what the flower would smell like. By doing this you are training your mind through your gaze to shift to the moment rather than cycle in the past (argument). As you gaze at the photo you allow your gaze to take in visions beyond such as your students, chairs, and desks. Your attention is being directed to your vision of the moment instead of to the past. Now, as you lift your gaze from your desk set your intention to notice something soothing before anything else. Perhaps gaze at the light coming in from the window or a student reading his book. Allow yourself to recognize that you have just reset your moment through the portals of your own eyes.

Your eyes are a resource for inner stability and calm. By closing your eyes, softening your gaze and planting visuals in your environment you are training your mind to go inward for peace. This makes you less reliant on circumstances or an environment that needs to be a certain way before peaceful moments are experienced.

Try This!

Practice Shifting Your Gaze. For one minute shift your eyes by scanning the room without moving your head around. Do this quickly, taking in every corner of the room. Pause and set your gaze on one thing for thirty seconds. Notice how shifting your eyes creates a shallow breathe and setting your gaze on one point deepens your breath.

Speech

Speech is your form of verbal expression. The quality of your words and how they are chosen can provide insight into how you are experiencing your world. The words you choose reflect your heart beat. If your heart rate is elevated, your words may be impulsive or quick. Words also often match your current mood. They have the ability to hurt or heal not just the individual you are speaking with, but yourself as well. Physiologically there is no difference between how the body receives what you say to others and what you say to yourself. If you say harmful things to yourself this may affect your health on a cellular level. The rule of thumb is less is more. Practice your speech. Rehearse how you speak to the student who drives you crazy. Role play and listen for your pitch, the emotional tone behind your words. Look at yourself in the mirror or talk to yourself out loud while driving your car. Watch and hear yourself say the student's name. Notice your tonality. A student's name is not just what you call them it is part of their vibration. If you are not aware, your tone of voice can come across as critical, sarcastic, negative, demeaning, or domineering. A tone can also be soothing, curious, confident, assertive, commanding, motivating, and humorous.

Your words are powerful. They represent how you express yourself in the guide role. The tone and fluctuation behind your words sends off an emotional signal. It may not necessarily be through what you say but rather how you say it that people find a way to connect to you. The connection keeps you aligned with your guide role.

Your Nose Knows (Olfactory system)

Your olfactory system, your sense of smell, is one of the most direct senses neurologically. Dr. Daniel G. Amen, a clinical neuroscientist who wrote the book, *Change Your Brain Change Your Life* states: "because your sense of smell goes directly to the limbic system, smells can have a powerful impact on the brain." He speaks of how "smell and memory are processed in the same area of the brain." Your sense of smell influences what you recall from memory as well as your mood. For example, imagine the smell of coconuts. I used to wear coconut oil and would constantly receive comments that I smelled like the beach. The coconut smell triggered memories and associations of the beach. Consider the smells that bring you peace, perhaps coffee brewing, flowers, apple pie baking, fresh clean laundry, and vanilla candles. I have a friend who is a realtor. She swears that it helps sell homes when she lights a scented candle creating the smell of apples or pumpkins. She also plays soft music in the background to give people a feeling of relaxation and connectedness.

Because smell is connected to mood, think about the impact some classroom smells have on you and your students. Anti-bacterial wipes, bleach, harsh perfumes, and musty rugs or corners are some smells that come to mind. Years ago, I received perfume for Christmas and decided to try it. I was driving in the car with my daughter and she asked, "What is that smell?" I told her it was my new perfume. She replied, "Open the windows it is giving me a headache." Needless to say I am now very conscious of what I choose to wear. The scent of lavender has been proven to support a calm mood. It is sold in many body care products, including bubble bath for babies, tea, and soap.

Consider looking around your classroom or work environment to see what smells you are exposed to on a daily basis. Talk to your students about the power of their sense of smell. Bring different smells into the classroom for them to try, such as pine cones, cinnamon, or apple cider. Ask them how the smell affects their mood and the memories they are able to recall. Experiment with your own mood by trying different scents on yourself. Some retreat centers actually prohibit the use of perfumes as it can trigger reactions in others. Perhaps the shaving cream you have been using for years is triggering anxiety more than calming you down. Or could a specific perfume be distracting to your students. Your attention to immediate smells may support a pleasant working environment where you and your students can feel focused and alert.

Ritualizing Taste

The way you approach meal time is an opportunity to empower you and your students. Ask yourself, *Is meal time (lunch) something to do, or is it a time to encourage responsibility, gratitude and self-reliance?* As the cost of living rises and the resources in our environment are depleted human beings are being called to action to give back to the environment and to learn how to become less reliant on others for their food supply. Schools are aligning with this by recycling, creating community gardens, engaging in community service, and turning to solar heating.

The national average amount of time students and teachers receive to consume their lunch is approximately twenty minutes, which includes travel time and wait time. Also, students across America are taking between seven and ten minutes to actually eat (*The Journal of Child Nutrition and Management*, 2002).

Think about the amount of times you have been rushed through lunch barely tasting, nonetheless smelling, your food. Rushing at meal time turns the act of eating into yet another experience to get out of the way, dismissing it as a routine rather than enriching it as a ritual. Experiences are rituals when they are repeated with an intention to connect to a greater ambition. Lunch time as a ritual inspires students using simple acts and moments of their day.

To alter lunch time from a routine to a ritual there needs to be a shift in perception. If lunch is viewed as an environment for promoting a sense of belonging, nourishment, and appreciation responses supporting that perception are more likely to follow. On the other hand, if meal time is pictured as crowd control, time management and in some cases a disruption, responses with a controlling nature may be preferred. Habitual rushing shrinks awareness. Educators can cultivate awareness during meal time by paying attention to how students are transitioned into the cafeteria. Welcome them with a smile, create small talk, laugh, arrange tables in a square or circle similar to a family meal, play soft music, offer thanks, and most of all breathe. Rituals have a celebratory feel, where routines tend to be more mundane. Ritualize the cleanup process by making it fun. Ask all the children wearing a certain color to clean up first, play music, or create special jobs for the students that are already done.

I realize this topic can feel like a dead end street because you are typically not the one who imposes the time line on lunch. However, your mindset and attitude toward meals can make a difference. I remember going to a conference and asking the person next to me if they had ever heard the presenter. She said," Yes, he is great. Plus he lets you out early so you can be ahead of the line for lunch."Obviously, not everyone can be first in line. However, when you allow time for you and your students to shift gears to prepare for lunch it makes a difference. It gives everyone a chance to clear their minds, become centered and interact with others.

Consider the following when turning on your taste buds in your guide foundation: try providing yourself at least a few minutes to transition into lunch mode. Consider taking meals outside on a nice day. Chew your food more and longer than usual. Just by chewing your food longer your breath will be deeper and you will receive an overall calmness. Give thanks for your food or offer thanks before eating a snack. Remember how blessed you are. Bring to mind all the people that needed to be involved to offer you the food on your plate, including the person who grew the food, how it was transported to you, the water and sun that nourished it, the workers and stores that supplied it. Treat meals as a ritual that connects you to your guide foundation and puts your guide vision into action.

The guide foundation is maximizing the use of your senses along with the power of intention to expand your potential. It is built on the small things in life; mealtimes, smelling the flowers, a hand shake, wink of the eye, and the sound of the rain. This foundation is completely within reach and can be obtained by anyone who is willing and ready.

Don't Step On the Cracks

While building your guide foundation, it is helpful to be aware of possible cracks along the way. This section reveals four areas that contribute to the formation of cracks in your foundation. Cracks are defined as moments of reactivity when mind and body separate. This separation translates as a feeling of unsteadiness or imbalance.

There is no perfect structure as cracks and maintenance is required. In this case the maintenance is your awareness. Awareness is what firms the foundation, diminishes the cracks, tones down reactivity, and creates inner balance. From a place of inner balance, your breath flows, thoughts are clear, and you are able to find a rhythm to your day. Think of when you were a child walking down the street playing, Don't Step on the Cracks or You Break Your Mother's Back. To play the game well, you needed to be focused. Focusing meant turning up the volume of senses visually and kinetically (how your body moves in space), and turning down your mental chatter. Essentially, your mind and body become one.

Use your awareness and focus to recognize the four areas that commonly cause cracks in your foundation. These include: personal triggers, the inner voice, a desire to fix, and self-compromise.

Personal Triggers

Personal triggers are moments when your feelings suddenly shift into reactive mode. These triggers are personal to you as they are often tied to memories, beliefs, and present and former thoughts of an unpleasant situation. Triggers are often activated by things you care about such as: respect, relaxation, and time. Examples of potential triggers in the classroom are: talking, bullying, tardiness, disruptions, poor effort, or anything that interferes with student learning. Triggers heighten your state of arousal. They tend to stimulate tension in your outer physical body desensitizing you from reading your internal bodily cues.

Your reactions toward your triggers create neurological grooves in the brain. Grooves are pathways, along which information travels from the brain, along the spinal cord, and through nerves that connect to your organs. When pathways are overused, grooves develop making it more likely for you to repeat the same reaction. When this happens, behaviors and thoughts start to cycle creating an automatic and repetitive response. The good news is that these pathways are not permanent. With patience and consciousness, new pathways form and with that come fresh responses.

Take note: What triggers you may not trigger someone else. Late buses, co-teachers calling in sick, loud students, tipping chairs, meetings that run too long, not getting enough done, too many rainy days may disrupt your sense of peace, but they may not trigger your colleagues.

> *Cindy, for example, prefers to show up early to set up for class. She aims to be prepared when students arrive. It also helps her to center herself. On this occasion, shortly before her students arrived, a woman came in rather disheveled to announce that Cindy had set up in the wrong classroom. The woman began to lay down her own materials as an obvious way to claim the territory. She then left to find a custodian to substantiate her story.*
>
> *The custodian returned with a clip board full of papers that indicated Cindy was in the wrong place and the woman was right. Cindy's personal triggers had been pushed. It was not the abruptness of the woman or the confrontation that triggered her. It was that her own preference for preparation was not allowed. Her learning style and temperament were not honored, causing her to lose her footing.*

Triggers create imbalance by heightening levels of reactivity. Reactivity is fueled by habitual response and a state of non-presence. One way to soften reactivity is to connect to your exhale. Take a long inhale and then on exhale counting backwards, five, four, three, two and one. At the end of the exhale, think of one word that could help you through that moment such as: tolerance, peace, and patience words that encourage relaxation. Take another long inhale and again, on exhale count backwards from five. Once you reach number one, repeat the word you choose. Do this three to five times either silently or out loud. This practice allows mind and body to work together while re-training the nervous system to allow a new response.

Intentional breathing is a tool that has been utilized by educational specialists such as: speech pathologists to benefit stuttering, teachers for behavior management, and counselors with problem solving for over a decade. When teachers devote themselves to intentional breathing they contribute to the process of self-actualization for themselves and those around them to an inner curiosity of their triggers and to the development of new neuro pathways for responding to them.

Try This!

Work with small triggers first. Small triggers are little annoyances that you notice but don't necessary get you fully off track. A small trigger might be the visual of a messy closet or an unorganized desk. It could also be what you say to yourself about that desk, *that desk is a mess or I need to clean that*. In order to work through the more intense triggers play with the small ones. For example, see the messy desk, hear the voice in your head, and then make the conscious choice to prolong your out breath (exhale 5,4,3,2,1).

Desire to Fix

A desire to fix is often a learned attempt to manage discomfort. Watching others muddle their way through frustration may bring up uncomfortable feelings such as confusion and concern in you. This may lead to responses that stem from a desire to fix, make the situation better, or in some cases go away. In the moment this desire may seem appropriate. However, it is important to be mindful of how discomfort is often the catalyst of inner growth.

I once consulted in a preschool classroom where a child had limited verbal skills, making grunting and high-pitched sounds to receive attention. The other children quickly saw how effective this was and decided to mimic the child. The behavior spread from one child to about five or six children. The teacher was desperate for help, could not take it anymore and only wanted to hear suggestions for making it stop. Unfortunately, this teacher needed to go through more frustration before recognizing that you don't fix children you connect to them. In fact, her strong desire to fix or change shut down her ability to consider any alternate solutions. As the consultant, I chose to remain in the guide role and prioritize my connection with the teacher. I could have easily gone down the same path, of wanting to change or fix this teacher. Instead I choose to listen and support her through questions that generate self-empowerment. I did so by asking her what is important to her as a classroom teacher. What is she choosing to cultivate in other words, her intention? I asked her to imagine the atmosphere she would like to see. Using language in the here and now, such as I see, I asked her to tell me the behaviors she would like to see instead. The teacher's answers became the guideline for creative solutions. For example, she identified the need for boundaries regarding people walking through the classroom or unexpected visitors. She connected this to her guide vision of describing her ideal classroom as a place of mutual respect, where people made appointments and provided warnings before dropping in. Through the process of asking questions, this teacher recognized that by over focusing on fixing the behavior, the real areas in need of attention became buried.

You can witness your students' desires to fix through behaviors such as constant tattling and approval-seeking. An example is the child that goes overboard as the teacher's helper. You may even see it in yourself as the mediator or the one to bring laughter to an uncomfortable situation. Perhaps it reveals itself through rigidity or over planning. When dominant, these responses provide a false sense of control, contributing to cracks in the guide foundation. Cracks however, can be sealed simply through activating your awareness. This may seem impossible to educators who are in charge of twenty plus students, however a feeling can be revisited at anytime. Your memories are connected to your sensations. This means your sensations of discomfort are available to you at any time. By seeking moments of stillness feelings of discomfort are given permission to surface and worked through. It is then that the clinging to counterproductive responses such as the desire to fix subsides. With that comes the stabilization of your guide foundation.

Try This!

Cover and press your right nostril. Did you know your left nostril is a direct connection to your parasympathetic nervous system? Some people refer to this technique as alternate nostril breath. Teachers can utilize this ancient technique as a way to move through the discomfort of triggers. Simply block your right nostril with your finger or thumb and breathe through the left nostril only for three cycles of breath (inhale and exhale are one cycle). Notice how this technique gives you access to the muscles and plexus of nerves in your lower back and abdomen.

From Self-Compromise to Compromise

> "I remember a veteran teacher stated at a staff meeting, "I hate that child!" When I did not stand up and say something, I compromised everything I believe regarding understanding children, individual development, and temperament" Cindy Horgan.

Self-compromise is putting your own needs and values aside for the sake of others. It is making a decision against your conscience the knowledge you have of yourself. Self-compromise in schools reveals itself at team meetings, parent meetings, and staff meetings, as well as through more casual discussions in the teachers' lounge. It tends to surface as a way to keep the peace or prevent conflict. As a school psychologist, I have experienced self-compromise as well as witnessed it. Saying yes when I really wanted to say no was one way I permitted it. Parents and teachers sitting idle when they really had something to say was a way I witnessed it.

When your goals outweigh or dominate the process, self-compromise steps in. The process of brainstorming, respecting differences, negotiation, self-inquiry, and listening is how self-compromise is transformed into compromise. Compromise is a skill focused on communication and respect. Compromise not only allows for differences but makes space for them as well. When there is compromise, people feel heard and respected, decreasing the need to or option of sacrificing your insight and potential.

Self-sacrificing behaviors such as putting aside self care and personal boundaries surface in situations where self-compromise exists. For example, sacrificing sleep for the sake of correcting papers or showing up at work sick rather than taking the time to rest. Pay attention to the individuals in your work environment that set boundaries and take time for self care. Ask them questions about how they balance personal and professional time and no doubt you will learn what they value. Educators influence each other just as much as they influence their students.

By drawing your attention to the process rather than over focusing on the outcome, self-compromise shifts into compromise. This means putting connection first. Compromise is a form of connection based on mutual respect and healthy communication. This can be applied individually as well as with others.

Try This!

Pay attention to agitation. Sitting in the teachers' room correcting papers may at times offer you balance or the reward of less to do at the end of the day. Other times it may be counterproductive making you feel exhausted or over worked. This can lead to irritability or a lack of motivation to take care of your own needs. Consider if you feel connected, motivated, or interested you are not compromising yourself for the sake of getting things done. However, if you are agitated or restless this may be a signal that your body needs to open up physically or in some cases spiritually. Physical responses are walking, stretching etc. Spiritual responses are getting outside with nature, breathing etc.

Hushing the Voices That Whisper

The voices that whisper are the inner voices that speak your truth. When heard, they give you insight into what is in your best interest. They are your personal post it message stating, remember you! Perhaps the doctor's appointment you have been postponing, a lunch date with a friend, putting off a vacation, or taking an exercise class. Like a small child tugging on your pant leg these voices are attempting to tug you toward your power.

Cracks form in your foundation of awareness when these whispers are pushed away or ignored. These cracks promote feelings of loss, not having enough, incompetence, and unworthiness. These same feelings draw on a negative state where self-defeating thoughts are permitted to surface. Thoughts such as: *I'm too old, I need to retire, things will never change or none of these kids know how to listen.* Consider that the thoughts that come back to you even after you push them away may be there for a reason. The reason, however, is not necessary to uncover. More importantly, learn to pay attention to the whispers without wanting or needing certainty from them. In other words, do what feels right as opposed to what you think you should do.

Resistance

Resistance is to stop, slow down, or prevent movement. Many times resistance is thought of as physical movement such as the resistance of lifting weights. However, in an educational setting resistance is intimately tied to emotional movement such as suppressing feelings, interest, or effort. Resistance keeps individuals from experiencing the discomfort of the present moment. When left unrecognized mental habits such as, thinking too much may be formed. These mental habits lead to the development of cracks in your guide foundation. The cracks are the symptom of the disconnection from your body and senses. For example, if you find yourself responding to a situation or student in the same way over and over again (e.g. verbal requests) despite its ineffectiveness you may be experiencing your own inner resistance. On the other hand, when you make the connection between what is happening inside of you and how it impacts your responses to others the cracks begin to seal themselves.

You may also witness resistance in your students. A student who is distracted and ignoring teaching direction may be resisting the moment. This may happen when material seems irrelevant or boring. The student may feel disconnected to how the material is being presented. Author Chris Howard speaks of resistance as a lack of rapport between individuals (pg. 144, 2004). In order to appeal to all learning styles and developmental needs the power of providing choices can never be underestimated. Choices invite students into a partnership where rapport and expectation can be developed together. The example below illustrates this further.

> *Picture yourself using the sole strategy of repeating verbal requests to students. You find some of the students are not responding. You raise your voice and speak louder. The students listen for a moment and then go back to the previous behavior. This triggers thoughts such as, the students don't listen (thinking). Your shoulders and chest become tense. However, you do not notice the tension because you are too busy looking (thinking) for what the problem could be. You start to feel annoyed by the amount of time the perceived behaviors are taking from the lesson.*

The above example illustrates three forms of resistance. First the teacher appeared to cling to one dominant strategy (verbal requests), two, she ignored her bodily tension and three she started to feel like she was losing something (time). Each of these are signs of resisting the moment. Now, imagine the teacher softening her resistance through her own awareness. She may respond to her bodily tension by rolling her shoulders, take a long inhale and a long exhale to help place herself in the present moment. These types of responses build rapport with your body first. When practiced regularly bodily rapport prepares you to notice the moment rather than search for a problem.

Space for creativity and fresh responses are created through you. Anything that inhibits awareness may leave you feeling confined, limited, or in some cases overwhelmed. By noticing your patterns of resistance, you free sensation, strengthening your skills as a teacher.

Don't step on the cracks reminding you to pay attention: listen, observe, and notice the influences on your guide foundation. Notice what thoughts and responses pull you away from your foundation and what keeps you connected. Pay attention to common cracks that show up in the form of personal triggers, your desire to fix, the times you self-compromise rather than compromise, inner voices that come in the form of a whisper, and finally, to resistance.

Try This!

Filter your perception. This technique was taught to me by psychotherapist Ana Zick. Imagine you have a screen in front of you. As you view what is happening in your classroom allow yourself to filter what information moves through the screen. Very often without realizing it teachers may mirror of what they see. For example, if they see distraction they may reflect that same distraction back to the students. In other words, you project distraction. Reflections add intensity to situations. By viewing yourself as a filter your experiences move through you smoothly without projection. You are then able to consciously choose what is being reflected.

CHAPTER 3

Emotions: Your Inner Guide

*"I've decided to stick with love, hates too heavy a
burden to bear" Martin Luther King.*

E MOTIONS DO MORE THAN TEACH you what your mood or feelings are.
They connect you to your heart and intuition, as well as your ability
to guide yourself and others. How you interpret and communicate your
emotions makes a difference with your teaching and overall well being.
Emotion comes from the Latin word *emovere* which means to move, to
excite or to agitate (preservearticles.com). Candace B. Pert refers to an
essay published in 1884 by a professor of philosophy at Harvard William
James. In his essay on emotions he stated that there was "simply perception
= bodily response." "The immediate sensory and motor reverberations
that occur in response to the perception-the pounding heart, the tight
stomach, the tensed muscles, the sweaty palms-are the emotions" (*Molecules
of Emotion*, Scribner, 1997 pg 135). The movement of your emotions and
sensations create a flow of energy. This flow ignites you with vitality, focus,
and resiliency. Your students receive the benefits by experiencing not

solely what you teach but may be empowered through your state of feeling. Feeling states that are heart based expand your ability to teach and reach students.

Accessing and Interpreting Your Emotions

Every emotion and situation has significance. How you interpret your emotions determines the relevance of information you receive. If you see your emotions as an asset the information received will have value. If you undermine or ignore your emotions the quality of information may be poor or impractical. Similar to a radio station, if you are having trouble discerning what you hear you are probably going to turn the channel. However, if the interpretation is useful and empowers you to make conscious choices you presumably will remain on the current station. When all emotions are permitted to move through your body you become more accessible to the ones that produce vibrancy and connection. Treating your emotions as sensations broadens your scope of feeling. For example, the simple urge to stop or ignore becomes part of the sensation rather part of the sequence that leads to an emotion. The urge *is* the emotion. Dr. Zoe Marae a biological scientist who did research at Harvard Medical School states: "it is not your emotions that are the problem, it is the non-movement of your emotions that can lead to disease." Her knowledge about the movement of emotions continues to have a profound effect on my teachings. She as well as other researchers taught me how to distinguish the difference between trying to move feelings and allowing them to move. Trying is highly connected to thinking while allowing feels quite effortless. To be effortless you must pay attention to your senses, skin cells and body parts including the heart center which supports the penetration of feelings. This section focuses on three matters. How to access your emotions, interpret movement and how the movement of your emotions strengthens your teaching and thus student learning.

Accessing your emotions requires an appreciation for how your emotions communicate through your body and mind. "Research in the new discipline of neurocardiology shows that the heart is a sensory organ and a sophisticated center for receiving and processing information. The nervous system within the heart (or heart brain) enables it to learn, remember and make functional decisions independent of the brain's cerebral cortex,"

Bradley, McCraty, & Tomasino, 2011. This research sheds light on the body and heart as a resource for accessing your emotions. In the past, science has been heavily focused on the brain as the control center for emotions. The brain, specifically the limbic system of the brain, does provide emotion. However the heart, nervous system and the gut (intestinal tract) also provide sensations and neurotransmitters which affect mood and the emotional read. The emotional read is the ability to identify and interpret your emotions.

In the guide role, interpretations that provide you information from both your mind and body are pursued. These interpretations are revealed through consciousness and awareness. It is your awareness that provides insight, wisdom, and direction. Interpreting is not to be confused with labeling the emotions. In fact, over-focusing on finding the correct label or meaning may misconstrue the message. To fully interpret an emotion, you must fully experience (move) the bodily sensations. Similar to reading, decoding the words properly is essential to comprehension. The beauty of experiencing your emotions is that you not only learn from your emotions but are also enriched by them. This enrichment loosens the strings of attachment from the state of doing to a state of being.

I once observed a teacher standing in front of her fourth grade classroom supervising her students while they sat at their desks eating cupcakes as part of a Halloween celebration party. She stood with a smile on her face watching the students interact and eat. As I watched her body I noticed her arms were crossed and her facial expressions fluctuated according to what was happening in the room. If the room became noisy her facial expressions reflected concern. Although there was nothing to do, I sensed the lack of structure in that moment was difficult for her. She appeared to fluctuate between frustration and ease. Now, imagine this same teacher standing in the room monitoring her students. Imagine her digesting her feelings rather than reacting from them. To digest her feelings she would need to stand tall and allow movement in her inner body. Perhaps expand her belly on inhale while softening her eyes on exhale. By doing so, she is making a conscious choice to value her sensations rather than react or attempt to control them. Children have many

*models of doing. Consider how they may respond to being. Perhaps
at first it may feel unfamiliar to be around someone who chooses to
be first. Yet over time as the unfamiliar becomes familiar students
learn and better yet witness the power of presence.*

Author Sarah Powers states awareness gives you the ability to "drop
thinking by choice, so you don't have to go down obsessive pathways."(*Insight
Yoga* workshop, July 28, 2012). Imagine being able to redirect students from
your bodily experiences opposed to your brain. By pausing and feeling you
experience. You are giving your brain a rest. Feel your skin, jaw, fingers,
palms, heart, mouth etc. Allow yourself to scan your body from inside
out, head to toe. Scanning your body is like checking yourself for a pulse.
This takes at most thirty seconds. The more you practice the more efficient
you become. Scanning your body lowers your reactivity and therefore
is best practiced before responding to your students. Most importantly
remember you are not searching for what is wrong. You are allowing yourself
to embellish in present sensations.

Try This!

Keep a soft belly. When scanning your body keep a soft belly. Remember
this area is a site for feel good hormones. Constricted bellies restrict breath
and inner movement.

Treat your sensations like you would a friend in need. Your attention is
another way of communicating, *I am here for you, I care about you, and I am
willing to listen.*

Interpretation

How you interpret your emotions alters your response to them.
Consider widening the viewpoint of what you think or believe. Consider
that your frustration is telling you to practice, slow down or be patient.
Sadness is often a communicator of pace, encouraging you to slow down,
rest, and contemplate. Fear provides alertness, intuition, and the ability to
act quickly. Anger reminds you what is important and when boundaries are
absent. Joy connects you to your purpose, your higher self, your reason for

being. Disappointment reminds you to let go and allow imperfections. Love provides empathy, freedom, understanding, and deep healing.

How you interpret your emotions influences what you receive from them. With awareness they are a means for support, encouragement, comfort, and direction. By pausing and feeling each emotion from the beginning, middle, to the end, you are allowing yourself to experience the benefits of your emotions.

TRY THIS!

How do you know you have experienced a feeling? If the numbers of thoughts have decreased and you are able to move on with emotions such as appreciation, gratitude, forgiveness, compassion or empathy for yourself and others then give yourself a pat on the back. You are learning to feel your feelings.

HOW EMOTIONAL FLOW STRENGTHENS TEACHING AND LEARNING

Similar to learning to read, moving your emotions requires readiness, maturity, and commitment. Using your emotions as a resource for inner guidance positively impacts your teaching skills. When your emotions become your inner guide you feel confident and less encumbered by the needs of others. Your students sense your comfort with yourself. This self-comfort sends a message of safety, security, and love. Students of all ages desire to be noticed, to belong, and to feel safe. It is through an atmosphere of trust, clear boundaries, and appreciation for differences that a student will flourish. The emotion of love is one of your most powerful tools for inner guidance. Love encourages you to see the good, empathize, accept, and encourage. When you hear yourself encouraging your students, good strategy, interesting idea, thank you, and I appreciate, you are sharing the emotion of love. Praise, on the other hand, can send the message, I approve of you. Praise sounds like, good boy, nice girl, I really like the way you etc. Praise tends to be a response from your brain more so than your heart. Brain responses may easily edge toward reactivity or even manipulation. Encouragement tends to have a more genuine, honest, and supportive quality. Anything that comes from the heart carries a strong vibration and benefits both you and your students.

One way to teach students about the value of their emotions is to share stories. Share stories about your emotions, where you felt them in your body, and how you choose to experience them. For example, you might share what it is like for you to take the teaching test. Describe your heart rate, sweaty palms, self-doubts, cold feet, and wide eyes. Share what you learned those emotions were telling you, why they existed and how you moved on. Perhaps your fear told you how hugely you wanted to be a teacher.

Cindy, the preschool teacher I spoke about earlier remembers volunteering to set up a display in the hallway at her children's school. There was not a lot of activity in the halls so she could easily hear teachers' teaching. In one particular class Cindy heard a sudden shift in rhythm. As she listened, a child become very agitated quickly and she could hear furniture moving in an odd way. As she traveled closer to the room with the intention of helping if needed, what she viewed was quite amazing. She saw a large child escalating in frustration and anger, a very petite teacher, and a room full of classmates. The teacher was the only adult in the room. What happened next left Cindy speechless. As the child escalated, the teacher clearly in her body opened her arms as she approached the child lowering her voice with each step to a calm tone. She walked slowly as if she were feeling her entire foot touch the ground before moving the other. The child, picking up on this energy began to de-escalate. Eventually, their tones matched as they moved into a rhythm of calmness. When their two energies joined the teacher privately pulled this child aside for problem solving. The entire class appeared to be grounded by the experience. The students smoothly transitioned back into the lesson. The following year Cindy requested that her child have that teacher. Her child did and the energy from this teacher carried to her entire family. In the story above, consciousness moved from the ground up meaning the teacher rooted herself in the moment by moving slowly, matching her tone and response to the pace of her body.

Through sharing stories, describing your emotions, using encouragement, positive interpretations, and movement of your emotions, you and your students learn how to create emotional flow. Emotional flow does not mean emotions are pouring out of you at all times. Emotional flow functions from the belief that your emotions are energy. Your awareness supports their capabilities. All emotions are valuable and capable of transforming your attitude, health, and response toward situations around you. When viewed in this way, students and teachers are more likely to take responsibility not only for what they feel but also for who they are.

TRY THIS!

Share tools. When sharing stories be sure to share the tools that got you through challenging moments. Include any self talk, coping, or focusing strategies including visuals that helped guide you through.

Keep your heart open. Close your eyes and take a deep inhale into the front of your heart expanding your belly and chest and a deep exhale into the back of your heart between your shoulder blades. If you are listening to your breath more than your thoughts you are in your heart.

Your Emotions Are Contagious

Emotions are catchy. Similar to a virus, they spread through classrooms, families, work environments, and relationships. The spreading of emotions is referred to as emotional contagion. Emotional contagion, is the tendency to catch and feel emotions that are similar to and influenced by those of others."(*The Free Encyclopedia, www.wikipedi.org*). Understanding and learning about emotional contagion decreases stress, diminishing classroom behaviors, while improving energy, focus, social responsibility, immunity, and overall attitude.

According to research lead by Hatfield and his colleagues, emotional contagion occurs most when there is a lack of awareness or consciousness. "Unpleasant emotions are more likely to lead to mood contagion, than are pleasant."Therefore, it is possible for your students to absorb and reflect your emotions. According to Bo Forbes, a clinical psychologist, anxiety is one of the most contagious emotions. Anxiety spreads through the widening of the eyes. If your eyes are wide, perhaps bulging, you are more likely to pick up the anxiety of others. Emotions are also contagious through tone of voice, volume or intensity of voice, non-verbal gesture, facial expressions, mimicking of others, attitude, pressure and more. Author Daniel Goleman, refers to a study in *Working with Emotional Intelligence*, where the most emotionally expressive person transmitted their mood to others in the matter of two minutes (pp.164). With awareness and effort you can buffer emotional contagion for yourself as well as your student.

> *When our daughter came home from middle school one day, I asked her about her day and also if she remembered to hand in the homework. She had spent several hours the day before drawing a detailed map. She replied, "Yes," and added that "The teacher was, "mad." I asked, "Why?" She said, "She was mad because not all of the students did their homework." She reported that the teacher said, "This is disgusting." I asked her if she too felt bad even though she had done her homework. She replied, "yes."*

This is an example of emotional contagion. Although my daughter did her homework, she picked up stress from her teacher. Research on short and long term memory show that stress hormones help "carve events into memory," (*Psych*, Rathus, 2009, p.152). This means my daughter's brain may store memories related to this event in her long term memory. This could increase the chances that she will associate certain things such as homework, social studies, or a specific teacher to stress. Stress, anger, and anxiety are highly contagious emotions. When contracted, the intensity limits the blood supply to the brain and body. This impacts you and your student's abilities to process, recall, and store learning. This is evidenced through poor communication, poor concentration, weakened immune systems, and loss of memory (i.e. recall, retention). Our quick paced lives have made it challenging to recognize where to draw the line. However, "stress is not just a problem of too much going on it is also about how well you attend to your emotions" (*The Open Focused Brain* by Les Fehmi and Jim Robbins 2007 pg.19). The teacher in the above example attempted to use her stress and anger as a means of communicating her standards. Emotions are a form of communication. A more effective response may have been for the teacher to:

» Take a moment to calm down.

» Read something inspirational.

» Jot down her angry thoughts on paper.

» Squeeze a stress ball.

» Take three long, three slow breaths, drawing out the exhale.

» Once calm, the teacher could have pulled the students who did not do their homework aside to speak to them privately and calmly.

» Finally, I am a huge fan of finding ways to motivate students to complete their work. One teacher increased homework assignments by telling his class if they did all of their homework they would go outside and play kickball on Fridays.

Your emotions are contagious. Talk out loud about this with your students. Let them know there may be times when you feel frustrated, angry, or stressed. Discuss ways of coping with emotional contagion when functioning in large groups. Bruna Martinuzzi, and Michael A. Freeman, M.D., authors of *The Leader as a Mensch: Become The Kind Of Person Others Want to Follow*, write about emotional contagion. Bruna states that emotional contagion can extend into the technology world. He cautions individuals to think twice before pressing the send button. Martinuzzi, suggests that you never give out criticism when you are in a bad mood. To lift your mood, he states: "focus on what you do best." Further ideas for decreasing emotional contagion in your classroom include:

» Allow time for creativity.

» Speak to students in private.

» Create opportunities for student mentoring.

» Offer breaks.

» Play upbeat music.

» Apologize for your mistakes.

» Interact with positive people.

» Write your thoughts down.

Emotional Restoration

Emotional restoration is the process of renewing your participation in your emotional well being through emotional movement. To fix means to repair, to restore means to bring something back to its original condition. Since emotions are energy in motion, restoring is the process of rejuvenating the flow of energy, rather than fixing your emotions. Energy cannot be fixed, it can only be influenced. The flow of movement is maintained through influences both in and outside of you. Some of these influences include: perception, awareness, muscular release, and self-monitoring of the senses. This next section is focused on the process of emotional restoration. It offers a deeper look at anger and fears two of the more challenging emotions. This is followed by ways to maintain emotional flow in your daily life.

Fear & Anxiety

Fear is an emotion generated out of danger when there is a real or perceived threat. Anxiety is fear of future events. Both of these emotions travel through the sympathetic nervous system sending your body into fight or flight mode. In fight or flight mode, your blood pressure rises, heart rate speeds up, muscles contract, and the brain is stimulated. The production of the stress hormone cortisol increases. If left unattended, high doses of cortisol lead to memory impairment, sleep disturbances, loss of energy, and other potential health hazards. Understanding fear and anxiety plays a crucial part in emotional restoration as the body does not differentiate between what is a real or imagined. For example, if you were correcting your students work and saw how poorly your students were doing, you may feel your heart rate increase, your eyes widen and your teeth clench. Perhaps you would start thinking anxious thoughts about how much work needs to be done before the year is complete. Your body may interpret your emotions as a potential threat (fear) or concern for the future (anxiety). If so, it would naturally protect itself by sending blood and oxygen to the major organs, away from the brain. This response fogs thinking, increases stress, and creates tension in your body. Although the threat is created by you, the body is not able to distinguish the difference.

The parasympathetic nervous system, on the other hand, is responsible for relaxation and inner calm. Both systems are built into each of us. M. NurrieStearns and R. NurrieStearns authors of *Yoga for Anxiety*, state, "The most obvious and immediate way to feel less anxious is by changing how you breathe."

TRY THIS!

Sit with your fear. During the times you feel fearful or anxious try consciously extending your exhalation. Begin by noticing the times your breath feels rapid or shallow. Perhaps times such as: teaching, prepping, correcting papers, administering a test, interacting with students, and staff. Sitting with fear is best practiced in situations where fear or anxiety may be only slightly elevated. To do this first acknowledge fear's presence in your body. Feel the sensations and allow them to move through you without acting on them.

In *Return to Love*, Marianne Williamson wrote: "Love is what we were born with. Fear is what we learned here." She states: "letting go means to just love." Fear is a part of the human experience and teachers have a front row seat to witnessing it in themselves as well as in their students. Fear and anxiety are evidenced through:

excessive nail biting	frequent absences
crying	distractibility
stomach ache	headaches
lack of motivation	negativity
perfectionism	poor sleep
anger	hypercritical
withdrawn	weak immune system
short tempered	

One of the most compassionate responses to fear and anxiety is to accept students for where they are in the moment, opposed to where you would like them to be. By accepting students for where they are today, a message of self-acceptance is encouraged. M. NurrieStearns, and R. NurrieStearns point out in their book *Yoga for Anxiety*, 2010, that believing you are flawed or less than others is a root cause of anxiety. To meet students where they are means to listen and observe. Observe when they need a break and listen for when they are asking to be challenged.

> *I once spoke with a fifth grade teacher who revealed she had a terrible fear of conflict. Whenever someone particularly a co-teacher was upset she would respond by saying something humorous. She used humor as a way to manage her fear around conflict. Her humor eventually became a cover up for her true feelings. Truthfully, she felt insecure about her ability to meet the demands of her job. Her humor served as a form of self-protection. Over time her body began to speak through a language of aches and pains. She eventually made the choice to retire early.*

Fear is what you learn. Fear separates the mind and body, love connects it. What you think, how you feel and how you respond directly affects your bodily responses. By becoming aware of these more challenging emotions you allow them to flow, illustrating to your students that feelings are nothing to be afraid of.

ANGER

Anger is a healthy emotion that most people experience on average a few times a week, Daw J. Holloway (*APA, March 2003, Vol 34, No. 3*). Anger is a difficult emotion to digest and is known to wreak havoc on the nervous system if left unattended. To leave it unattended means to lack awareness or the skills for working through an emotion. Students and educators need support when their anger negatively affects learning and teaching. In the process of emotional restoration, less emphasis is placed on preventing the emotion while more attention is given to finding constructive ways to experience anger.

The purpose of this section is two-fold to provide insight on what your anger as well as the anger of your students may be telling you, and to bring awareness to how teaching and honoring emotions works in favor of learning potential.

Before age nine, boys, and girls show their anger quite easily. As society begins to send the message that anger is bad, children are left to figure out what to do with this natural emotion. Girls often choose to hide it while boys may choose to misplace it. Hiding or misplacing an emotion is a temporary solution. Anger will eventually seep out of its hiding place at times in self destructive ways. Gossip, passive aggressive behavior such as sarcasm, and eye rolling, negativity, body image dysfunction, criticism, and avoidance are some common ways anger seeps through. Misplaced anger may show up through aggression, blame, and self-destructive behaviors such as drugs and alcohol. Students learn to hide their true feelings out of fear that they will jeopardize what other people think of them. Students and staff hide feelings when there is a lack of trust or open communication. When feelings are hidden or misplaced it leads to confusion about which feelings are real and which are pretend. Overtime, this confusion creates a disconnection from true self, strengthening a false sense of self.

Anger sends the message that something you care about has been violated in some way. It most often indicates that a personal boundary has been crossed. Anger is tricky because it is typically a secondary emotion, meaning you may feel another emotion first such as frustration or hurt. Anger has similar sensations as frustration including increased heart rate and muscular tension. However, because society views anger as a problem it tends to become hidden behind the shadows of frustration. People are less likely to admit their anger and more likely to interpret it as frustration. The challenge then becomes learning the message. Frustration sends the message to slow down, practice and be patient. Anger sends a different message of the need to set healthy boundaries. Beverly Engel states, "People who use anger well understand that the purpose of anger is to solve problems, not just to ventilate their feelings" (*Honor Your Anger: How Transforming Your Anger Can Change Your Life*, 2004, pp. 93). When you hear from a parent that a child is angry about school, that is an indication that a boundary is lacking. Homework is an example where students can feel angry due to the loss of personal time or a personal boundary that separates work and play

TRY THIS!

Post a sign on your wall that says, "All Healthy Expressions of Feelings Are Welcome Here." Ask students to describe healthy expressions of anger, fear, anxiety, or embarrassment. Set clear guidelines for when and how to talk about emotions. Create an environment where students witness healthy expressions in each other. Talk about frustration and anger as if you were talking about what you were going to have for lunch. Normalize it make it familiar, natural, and comfortable.

What is my intention? Ask yourself this question when you become angry. Very often anger is connected to what someone else is or is not doing. By tuning into your intention you reconnect to your heart, the place that reveals the truth about what is behind the anger.

Maintaining Emotional Flow

Emotional restoration is the rejuvenation of your emotional energy. You do this by maintaining your emotional flow, the movement of your energy. By maintaining emotional flow you are conserving your energy, passion, and personal power. The section below reveals simple ways to emotionally restore yourself throughout the day. You will notice that each suggestion impacts your body by circulating your blood, lowering blood pressure, increasing oxygen to the brain, and stimulating feel good neurotransmitters. These are key components to creating emotional flow, leading to emotional restoration. You can utilize these suggestions yourself or with your students.

Smile

Your smile has the ability to lift your mood as well as the mood of others. It represents your uniqueness and grants you the ability to connect and bond with others. Your mouth contains as much as fifteen smile muscles. How many you contract depends on how expressive your smile is. A smile that squints the eyes and lifts your eye brows will contract more muscles than a smile that does not. When you smile, it is similar to closing your fists tightly and releasing them. Smiling lifts your jaw and lower lip and when released relaxes the muscles engaged. Your jaw is highly connected to worrying. When you worry, most often the jaw and smile muscles tense up. Relax your jaw, relax your tongue, relax the corners of your mouth, relax your upper and lower back teeth and your mind will relax. Smiling is a built-in remedy for combating anxiety and stress. Emily Zhivotovskaya states: "When you smile at someone else, they smile and you are causing physiological changes within their bodies" (article written in *positivepsychologynews.com* 2008). Her article reported findings from Dr. Mark Stibich: smiling boosts the immune system, increases positive effect, reduces stress, lowers blood pressure, and enhances other peoples' perception of you. Students who receive your smile are more likely to feel comfortable with a positive connection to you. You can also utilize your smile while engaging in activities that may be stressful such as grading or report writing. Your smile softens any experience, lifts your attitude, and increases your effectiveness in communicating with others.

Laughter

Laughter is a built in automatic behavioral response that contracts many of your smile muscles. Laughter can be contagious. It has the power to elevate your mood and lighten the atmosphere in the room. A silly picture, joke, or gesture can impact perception, lift mood and help you and your students to move feelings. An article posted on CNN written by Brigid Delaney, *The Benefits of Laughter*, reported a study researched by The

American College of Cardiology (*articles.cnn.com*, 2011). The study found "the positive effects of laughing lasted for up to 45 minutes while in contrast the effects of stress decreased the blood flow by 35%." When you laugh your blood flows more freely, supplying your body with more oxygen and naturally releasing your feel-good hormones. This blood flow plays a big part in your emotional restoration. One way to encourage more laughter is to start with yourself. Make mistakes safe by laughing at yourself. Share your silly screw ups, tell a joke, hang up a silly poster, watch a funny movie, or share a story. I once asked my daughter about her day at school. She shared a story of how her teaching was tugging on her own turtle neck, sticking out her tongue, panting like a dog indicating to another teacher she felt hot. Out of all the things in the day this is what my daughter remembered and connected with the most.

Laughter increases your blood flow while connecting to the movement of your emotions. The movement transforms into energy of a higher frequency where emotional connection and joy are stimulated. Appropriate laughter meaning laughter that does not hurt anyone else is a sign that you and your students are in the moment, in other words, in your power.

Keep Breathing

Breathing is the processing of taking air into the lungs. On inhale taking air in oxygen is taken into the lungs. On exhale (breathing out) carbon dioxide is released out of your lungs. Your lungs are located in your chest and take up quite a bit of space. Underneath your lungs is a muscle called the diaphragm. With breathing exercise, this muscle regulates the quality of your breath. The lungs are protected by your rib cage which has attachments to your spine. Therefore keeping the spine supple assists the development of breathing. The deeper and slower the breath the easier it is to fine tune breath consciously connecting to nerves that calm you in the lower lobes of the lunges. Deep slow breathing allows you to remove old, stagnant air. It is similar to walking into a room that has been closed off for quite some time. The air smells, stagnant, old, and dirty. The lungs are your windows letting in fresh oxygen, releasing old air, renewing your overall health, and emotional outlook.

Fine tuning your breath supports the process of emotional restoration. Once you fully understand your breath you become more confident in not only utilizing it but teaching it to your students. Studies have proven working with the breath provides many benefits to you and your students including:

boosts immune system	clears the mind
tunes you into your sensations	fosters self-awareness (power),
improves memory,	elevates mood
decreases pain	slows down aging
reduces stress	

Effective breathing offers calmness, connection, strength, and stability. "It is well known and widely accepted that your breath and your mental states are closely related." R. Rosen (pg. 36). Rosen speaks about the effects of shallow breathing primarily in the chest especially the reduction of carbon dioxide in the body, which constricts blood vessels, slows down circulation, excites the sympathetic nervous system, and places you in a state of fight or flight (pg. 22).

The first step to encouraging proper breathing is to encourage yourself as well as your students to sit up tall. Just by making the spine vertical, rather than slumped, you invite positive emotions to surface. Rosen states, "The spine isn't just a physical structure it is a psychological one as well."(pg.102). Once the spine is erect, put your hand on the lower half of your abdomen. On inhale, push your abdomen into your hand as if you were filling up a balloon with air. On exhale press your navel toward your spine while keeping the spine vertical. It naturally wants to slump on exhale. Try lifting your rib cage on exhale as if you were puffing out your chest to retrain your muscle to lift during both the inhalation as well as the exhalation. Some more subtle ways to encourage breathing is to soften the tongue in your mouth, relax the corners of your mouth, and set your gaze on the floor, several feet in front of you. Erect spine, soft gaze, lifted ribs, and connection to the lower belly all are key teaching points for illustrating proper breathing.

In 2010, I started facilitating empowerment groups for girls ages eight plus. The groups are often rich with discussion about feelings. The girls offer examples of feeling hurt, angry, or embarrassed. Girls tend to hide these more challenging emotions as a way of protecting their good girl image. I have learned from running these groups that it is not necessary for me to give the girls the answers. Providing a safe space where girls can express and restore their emotions is enough. It is from a place of emotional restoration as well as the exploration of self-expression that girls will learn how to speak up for themselves. By teaching girls how to breathe I am providing the foundation for problem solving and growth. To expect girls to be able to problem solve without emotional restoration may set them up for disappointment and perceived failure.

Proper breathing positively affects your psychological, physical, and emotional well being. Practice on yourself first to find ways to naturally bring it into your curriculum. Once you personally feel the effects, you will want to share it with your students. When done regularly the benefits are experienced almost immediately taking only seconds of your day. Try dedicating thirty seconds to proper breathing every hour before beginning or when ending a task. It is one of the simplest ways to encourage movement of emotions for you and your students. This movement provides the insight and strength necessary for problem solving.

Light

Exposure to sunlight and fluorescent lighting can either restore or deteriorate your emotional energy. A limited 15 to 20 minutes daily amount of sunlight restores your emotional balance by triggering your body to produce vitamin D and the chemical serotonin. This elevates your mood, evens bodily levels, including temperature and blood pressure and has been linked to prevention of heart disease. However, according to Mark Winterbottom of Cambridges faculty of education, "there is enough evidence that equipment (i.e. overhead projectors, computers) coupled with excessive fluorescent and natural light can cause headaches and impair visual performance"(*Child Health News*, 2007).

The sympathetic nervous system (fight or flight) can be activated through the overuse of computers, overhead projectors, and fluorescent lighting. Some individuals are more sensitive than others. One way to recognize if you or your students have activated your sympathetic nervous system is through observation of pupil dilation, tension or sweating. Computers, overhead projectors and fluorescent lighting are a huge part today's educational environment. It is important to check in with yourself and your students periodically. By asking whether they prefer to have the lights off or on you are encouraging them to check inward and advocate for their own well being. A time to consider checking in is when students return from computer class.

Physical education and health teachers have the advantage of being able to expose students to sunlight more frequently by going outside. It is important to tell students why you are making the choice to do so. Teach students about the effects of sunlight on mood and how it is important to balance the amount of screen time in your day. The term screen time includes all electronic devices such as televisions, phones, computers, and overhead projectors. Staff can enjoy the benefits of sunlight by going outside for lunch. By placing a staff picnic table outside, administrators can encourage this effort.

The monitoring of artificial light and the encouragement of natural sunlight supports the process of emotional restoration. The use of electronic devises support teaching and learning. However, it is important to self-monitor and ask for student feedback. The feedback you receive provides great insight into whether emotions are being restored or impaired.

Try This!

Check in questions. To see where students are at emotionally ask questions such as:

- » How is your breathing?

- » How are your eyes?

- » Do you need a brain break?

- » Roll your shoulders and tell me if your body feels loose or tense.

Sleep

A healthy night of sleep can restores you emotionally, intellectually, and physically. The National Institute of Health defines sleep as: "biologically motivated behavior."It states "adequate amounts of sleep dependent on age and temperament are necessary for normal motor and cognitive functions." Sleep is a well researched topic. There seems to be a consensus that the amount of sleep one needs varies depending on the individual. A regular, consistent sleep / wake cycle seems to provide the most benefit. This means going to bed and waking up around the same time every day. As little as one hour less of sleep can lead to irritability, lack of patience, weakened immune system, conflict, and slower processing. Symptoms of students with ADHD exacerbate with lack of sleep. Ronald E. Dahl, M.D. in the article, *The Consequences of Insufficient Sleep for Adolescents,* discusses studies that were done on groups of adolescents. One of the findings reported that it is better to get regular consistent sleep through a regular sleep/ wake cycle than it is to try to sleep longer to make up for missed sleep. R. E. Dahl states: "Insufficient sleep can amplify emotional difficulties, which can then produce further sources of distress and increased disruption of sleep." The article demonstrates how poor or lack of sleep impairs motivation (difficulty initiating tasks), increases negative mood and negatively impacts attention, behavior, and memory.

The National Institutes of Health lists **misconceptions** about sleep. A reprint of these misconceptions can be found at www.sleepdex.org/ misconception.htm. Some of the misconceptions include: "the body adjusts to different sleep schedules" "people need less sleep as they grow older," "getting just one hour of less sleep per night will not have an effect on daytime functioning."

Sleep offers emotional stability and restoration. Sleep brings you into another state of awareness allowing you to process your emotions through dreams. Consider asking your administration to educate families about the benefits of a good night sleep. Teachers can support this effort by assigning homework that calms the body down such as reading. I would avoid giving homework assignments such as practice tests or assignments that take an unreasonable amount of time to complete. A wind down routine before sleep is just as important as sleep itself. It can make difference between a restful or restless night.

Food

The relationship between what you eat and how you feel is significant. Without awareness of the food mood connection, the process of emotional restoration will be challenging and perhaps at times disappointing for you. Despite the work I have done in the last ten years studying the mind/ body relationship, it was not until I became educated in food that I was truly able to restore myself emotionally. Until then I was working primarily off will and intellect. Once I started to modify how I eat, the mind, and body worked effortlessly together. Like your emotions, food is another form of energy.

Enter any teacher's lounge and surely you will find sugary food items along with distribution of baked goods. I remember stimulating myself mid-day as a school psychologist with a can of diet soda and a handful of Hershey kisses from the receptionist's desk. I did not dare put them on my desk but I knew where they were when I was desperate for a sugar kick. Jack Challem, author of *The Food-Mood Solution*, writes about the relationship between food and mood. He states: "Your body needs vitamins, protein, and other nutrients to make the brain chemicals that help you think clearly, maintain a good mood and act in socially acceptable ways."(pg.5). Countless studies have been conducted on high blood sugar levels leading to conflict, irritability, angry outbursts, and impaired memory increase. Challem, refers to food with "neuronutrients" which are "needed to make neurotransmitters. Neurotransmitters, in turn, are the chemicals that control mood"(p. 4).

Educators and staff can support one another by encouraging a culture where low sugar foods are provided. Consider sharing soups, brewing herbal tea, placing vegetables, or salad on the staff table. As individuals, consider decreasing the amount of sugar in your diet. In addition, keep yourself well hydrated. If you are not urinating regularly you are most likely not hydrated. I am writing this piece during the week of Thanksgiving. Remembering how sugar truly affects my moods I am preparing a healthy soup which can contribute and will fill me up so I don't overindulge in desserts. Most likely in your area you can find someone talking to or working with people about food. A nutritionist or health coach may be ways to jump start this effort. I can't emphasize enough how much I believe in the food mood connection.

Power is the recognition that you have the built-in ability to restore yourself emotionally. This is done through the process of creating emotional flow. When emotions are flowing, the body restores itself rhythmically through circulation, production of glucose, cellular turn over, feel good hormones and fresh oxygen. This resets your rhythm waking up any sensations that lie dormant within you. Sensations that are pushed aside for the purpose of taking care of everyone else's needs are no longer desirable in this state. Emotional restoration soothes the inflammation of reactions that no longer serve you instead producing the inward shifts that percolate true power.

CHAPTER 4

Modifications for Observations

CHAPTER FOUR OFFERS MODIFICATIONS FOR observing yourself and others. Similarly to your modification of a student's work, this section offers ways to connect to your true potential in the absence of unnecessary distress. As you incorporate the modifications your sense of self boosts your ability to work with your students. In the end, your mind and body are rewired to respond in ways that are mutually favorable.

REVERSE

Reverse is about learning to observe yourself first. It is not uncommon for teachers to observe or notice their students' behavior before they study themselves. By observing yourself first you are less likely to think and more likely to feel. When you think more than feel, you are setting yourself up for a possible reaction to what you see going on around you including the conduct of your students: how they move about the room, their work habits, abilities, and social interactions. A typical reaction may be to think how what you see is impacting others and what needs to be done to stop it.

Reactions feel like refereeing. They fire off quickly in attempt to stop the game abruptly. They interrupt teaching. Reverse is about noticing yourself first, you might ponder a thought, feeling your way towards a response. By doing so you are more likely to maintain the flow of your teaching while contributing to any shifts that promote emotional balance.

In this chapter, see the benefits of observing yourself first. Understand what mindful observations are and how to apply them to yourself as well as your students. Note the difference between observing for data collection and mindful observation. Finally, learn how observing yourself first benefits everyone.

> *The voices in the classroom are getting louder. You look around the room and see students talking across the room, chairs tipping and bodies moving. Immediately you think to yourself, It is too loud in here, no one is working, I need to do something. As you walk over to the light switch to turn off the lights and raise your voice you notice the pitch of your voice is higher. Your heart rate is elevated but you simply ignore that, since you have a bigger task at hand. You need to calm these kids down before they disrupt the other classes.*

You First

Self observation is an intentional act. It is not the same as ignoring or disregarding what is going on around you. It is a way to cultivate responses from consciousness. Your inward preparation cannot help but influence how you respond to others. By noticing what is happening inside of you, you are inevitably supporting the growth of both you and your students. True growth is less dependent on whether the outcome is good or bad. When true growth is stimulated it is often experienced as an inward shift. This is similar to the feel of a a ha! moment when a student masters a skill.

Self observation is like taking the lens of a camera and looking inward. If you were to look within you may notice sensations. Your pulse, heart rate, the urge to do something say something, or bodily tension. Noticing what is happening inside you frees you. Ignoring or distracting yourself from inner experiences may limit you. Instead, you are confined or dominated by external perceptions, or misconceptions. Inside views multiply your tools, knowledge, and resources. These are your feelings, awareness, and connection to the present moment. Reactivity leads to physical and mental exhaustion. By placing yourself first your teaching becomes a natural flow of teachable moments.

Try This!

Observe the location of a feeling. Notice the places in your body your sensations get shut off and where the sensations are firing off. Watch how sensations of fear and excitement may be difficult to decipher. It does not matter which is which. What matters is you notice the sensations.

Mindful Questions

Mindful observations begin with mindful questions. By asking yourself questions you are redirecting your attention to yourself. The following questions will help you with this process. In the beginning it may feel awkward to ask yourself questions. Over time it will become more comfortable. Refer to these questions when you find yourself habitually observing your students *before* yourself.

Please note: If you find your breathing is shallow or limited, you feel little to no sensation, and your thoughts are firing than you may be in reactive mode. No worries, this knowledge about yourself is a gift. You are just a few breaths away from moving into responsive mode.

» How is my breathing?

» Do I feel sensation?

» Are my thoughts increasing?

» What does my body need to allow this moment?

Try This!

Develop your gaze. Begin by finding something in your classroom you can visually gaze at. It can be anything, as long as it is a few feet in front of you and preferably on the floor. A plant, book, a crack on the floor it does not matter. Looking at something on the floor forces you to lower your eyes, toning down reactivity. Take one long inhale and one long exhale while gazing at this point. This should take no more than five seconds. If you are beginning to think less and feel more consider yourself to be in a responsive mode. Watch and ask yourself how your responses may have altered. Has the tone of your voice changed, choice of words altered? Has the speed of your response slowed? Your students reflect how you are experiencing the moment.

It Only Gets Better

Mindful observations help you to see situations more clearly. Clarity allows you to release responses that are no longer effective or beneficial. Each time you release old perceptions you make room for new ones. Your perceptions have the potential to transform relationships, freeing your mind from unnecessary clutter.

In *The Curse of the Good* Girl, Rachel Simmons cites the work of Dr. Aaron Beck. She states: "Beck observed that when people were upset, they were more likely to incorrectly interpret others as being upset. He further saw that once people made assumptions, they became irrationally convinced that their guesses were absolute fact, even when they had no proof," (pg. 38). Mindful observations de-clutter your mind from making quick assumptions as well as from taking things too personally. For example, you may feel paranoid or concerned that students are talking about you. You become cluttered by thoughts of needing to control, fix, or figure out whether it is true. This may lead to quick action such as making demands or giving lectures, both of which are a form of disconnection. By redirecting your attention to your breath, you tone down the intensity making it more likely that you will choose responses of connection. Perhaps speak to the student privately or use humor to break possible tension. For younger students at preschool level, I have seen cluttered minds lead to the dismissal of feelings. Adults may do this through stating you are fine, instead of listening to and validating how the child feels. These statements typically occur when people feel rushed or unsupported.

Mindful observations are like fine wine, they improve with age. The more you practice mindful observations the better you feel. The better you feel the more adept you are with your students. You feel yourself flow from one thing to the next with more ease. The ease comes from catching and watching the tension early on. It no longer has to accumulate or scream at you through various bodily symptoms before you notice it.

Try This!

Spring clean your mind. Treat your cluttered mind like a spring cleaning. Each time you *allow* yourself to notice your breathing you are creating space between thoughts. This space makes room for connection and creative thinking.

Practice observing yourself as often as you can. The best way to build the skill of mindful observation is through attention to some of the ordinary moments of your day. Pouring a cup of coffee, walking across the room, and sitting in your chair are a few examples. Each time you notice yourself you become infused with presence, a place where anxiety cannot grow. Do this by noticing your senses and bodily movements. How does the temperature of the cup feel in your hand, the weight feel in your feet? Notice the texture of the chair. See if you pay attention to only certain parts of your body and not others.

Complete one task at a time. Multi tasking can be much like a form of distraction. Consider putting away or completing one task before moving on to another.

Notice your finger tips. Your finger tips have many condensed nerve endings which help you to direct communication from the body to the brain as opposed to from the brain to the body. In other words, you give your brain a rest by communicating to your nervous system through your body. Notice how your finger tips feel as they pick up a piece of paper, tap the keys on a keyboard, or pick up a cup of hot tea.

I Think You're Alone Now

One of the best times to practice self observation is when you are alone in your classroom. You may be surprised to discover how much bodily discomfort you feel. Moving these feelings is a visceral experience meaning your attention is moving the energy of discomfort through your internal organs and spine. During the day you are most likely too busy or distracted to notice your own bodily sensations. The only way to experience relief from this discomfort is to actually feel them. It is much easier and realistic to begin this process when you are alone.

Find a moment to sit comfortably in your classroom *alone* with the lights off. This will only take a few minutes. Pick a time of day when it is least active in the school building. Sit up tall and place both feet firmly on the floor approximately hip width apart. Once your feet are firmly planted on the floor begin to relax your shoulders. Relax your hands. Allow your chin to be level with the floor and press your head back gently so it is directly stacked in line with your spine. Begin by taking three to five long breaths inhaling and exhaling. Notice any subtle shifts in your skin. Do you feel tingly or a gentle pulsing sensation on your skin? As you move into this heightened state scan your body from head to toe. Do this with your eyes closed or with your gaze lowered toward the floor. Your breath is your internal motor it keeps the scan active and your mental acuity. Draw your attention to different areas of your body. Notice your feet, shins, knees, thighs etc. all the way to the top of your head. This can be done in seconds or minutes whatever feels comfortable for you. Refrain from feeling rushed instead explore the motion of thoughts such as, *am I doing this right?* It is as if you are running your body through an internal X-ray machine. Once complete, open your eyes and begin to look around your classroom. Notice what you see, hear, and feel. Notice the shadows in the room, the space between desks the piles of paper, light coming through the window, colors on the floor, sounds in, and outside the room. Just notice. How has your response to what you see shifted? Before the scan you may have had thoughts such as: *I need to clean that corner or I forgot call Jamie's mother back.* If you wish to deepen or provide additional support for yourself consider keep a journal of your thoughts, impressions, and feelings from these experiences.

TRY THIS!

Treat your classroom like a sanctuary. Take advantage of the quiet moments. Find a place in your room that is away from electrical devices such as computers, near a window, or plant. Turn off overhead lighting. Don't be surprised if these practices lead you to make some constructive classroom changes such as the re-organization of furniture or materials.

TIME FOR CLASS

Now that you have observed yourself in your classroom *without* students, it becomes a lot easier to observe yourself *with* students present. There is no right or wrong way to do this. It is simply an exercise, allowing you to familiarize your sensations in different situations. Each process connects you to the bigger picture, which is to transform any sensations formally experienced as reactivity into higher consciousness. Your higher consciousness is your responsiveness, knowledge, and wisdom.

Observing yourself with your students is a continuation of self observation in the presence of your students. Begin the process by making a personal agreement to let go of any judgments or strategies. You are not evaluating how your students make you feel. Your students are simply a reflection of what you may have already been feeling. What matters is your attention to this moment.

> *As you walk around your classroom notice the sounds. Notice which sounds are nearby and which are further away. Notice the sounds of moving chairs, pencils, erasers, whispering, or feet tapping. If you start thinking thoughts such as, that sound is annoying or Joseph isn't working you are no longer observing. You are thinking. As this occurs, gently bring yourself back to simply observing. Notice the colors, the shadows, and the temperature of the room. Notice your breath and how it flows in one nostril and out the other. Are you holding back your breath? Continue observing for thirty to sixty seconds. Then pause and notice if you feel any different.*

When done regularly, this exercise offers you many benefits. It teaches you how to relax your body in an atmosphere of potential stress. Toning down reactivity in the classroom cannot be done solely on intellect or willpower. The time to teach your mind and body to be calm in the classroom is <u>not</u> when you are in the heat of the moment. Non-reactivity is best taught during the more ordinary moments of your day. Consider implementing this during some of the natural pauses of your day when you students are occupied with work or before you begin or end a task. If a student approaches you while you are observing yourself, nudge your attention to observe the student in front of you. Note the student's facial expressions or the color of his shirt. If you find yourself thinking, gently draw your attention to the space between your eyes. This may help sway you back to the present moment.

Try This!

Regulate test taking. Next time you are proctoring a test engage in mindful observations. This places your attention on promoting a calm atmosphere opposed attempting to control what could be considered out of control. Instead you are choosing to send out signals of comfort and ease. This way you become order instead of attempting to keep order

How Mindful Observations Differ From Data Collection

Mindful observations differ from data collection. They lack a specific agenda, judgment, goal, or purpose. Observing for data collection typically is for gathering information for future reference or decision making. You may observe a student for the sole purpose of deciding whether his or her seat placement is appropriate. Perhaps he or she is having trouble seeing, hearing, following along, or staying focused. A focused assessment and evaluation of the situation is necessary to make the right decision. Perhaps the student works best in smaller groups or in a seat furthest away from the door.

Mindful observations differ in that they feed you with the benefits of experiencing the present moment. They reduce stress and promote an atmosphere of safety and security.

Observations for data collection are ways to collect evidence and support for future decisions about the educational needs of your students.

Try This!

The best way to know the difference between mindful observations and observing for data collection is to experience it. Take a situation where you observe a student and collect data on what you see for example, number of times a student makes an error while reading a small passage. Ask the student to read it again. This time observe the student mindfully. Without evaluating or correcting notice the students body language, the way he scans the page or the colors in his shirt. Just notice. See if you *feel* the difference between the two styles of observation.

Observing Student Behavior

Mindful observations provide you with a clear view of the workings behind student behavior. Often there are subtle movements that take place before a behavior occurs. When you mindfully observe a student's body before he talks out of turn you may ascertain how his impulse traveled. Impulse and distraction often begin in the feet. Watch your students feet tap and wiggle. Now imagine a student who bounces his knees up and down. Is the student bored, confused, irritated, distracted, or impatient? Mindful observations not only tell you about the student but also give insight into your reading of the situation. What assumptions are you making? One person may view a bouncing knee as anxious or distracted while another may view it as a tool for remaining on task. How you interpret the behavior has a great deal of influence on how you respond.

Rather than make careless assumptions consider these observations a doorway for communication. Ask Jimmy what his body is trying to say as he bounces his knee while working. What words or thoughts come to mind when he bounces his knee? There is no right or wrong answer you are trying to guide the student to make a connection between his inner and outer world. Don't be concerned if a student cannot answer. Don't become pre-occupied with the bouncing knee. Tune into the times the student is fully engaged. Perhaps the knee bouncing does help the student to engage however, on average people tend to absorb information better when they are comfortable and emotionally connected. I find some students need to move before this can occur. Once you see and feel the student's sense of focus you are then able to point this out to the student as it is occurring in your body as well as theirs. This makes your job easier as students shift their ways from feeling rather than doing.

Watch the difference between hands on instruction and independent seat work. Mindful observations are less about doing and more about watching. It is not about comparing one student to the next. The emphasis is on noticing the unique relationship between body and mind. When practiced regularly the observations lead you to long term solutions. A long term solution in this case would be the student making the connection between bouncing his knee and holding his breath.

Try This!

Notice how you feel when you redirect. Many times students are redirected once they push a teacher's button or push the limits. The moment you feel the slightest constriction in your chest, elevation in your heart or piecing lips, direct your awareness to the area of your body where you feel the most sensation. The top of your head including hair, jaw line, or skin on your face may feel more alive than other parts of you. By tuning into the sensation you are indirectly asking your awareness to grow. From this heightened state begin to redirect your students. Notice if how you chose to redirect alters. Perhaps you move closer to the student or you are able to make changes that reduce the need to redirect such as seat changes.

Try This!

Direct students to their breath. Have your students breath while gazing at a focal point. Chose something in the room for students to set their eyes on, ring a chime, and ask students to passively watch their breath for twenty seconds twice a day. Teach them how to notice the sound of someone walking in the room, or pencil sharpening through a state of awareness rather than reactivity. For example, have your students retrain themselves to breath rather than turn their head to see who is sharpening their pencil. This practice teaches students how to focus in the environment they are expected to focus in.

Insert name. One way to redirect students back to task is to insert their name playfully into your lesson. For example, Sam goes to the store with five dollars to purchase milk.

Non-verbal redirection. A light touch on the shoulder or tap on a student's desk continues to effectively redirect student behavior.

Introducing Mindfulness to Your Students

Schools are gradually becoming more open to the benefits of introducing mindful programs to students. I have seen some programs that have worked well. Others quite frankly turn students off. I am cautious about cookie cutter or one size fits all approaches. Like a good teacher, you must be able to adjust your style to meet the needs of the students and the teachers.

Introducing mindfulness requires everyone involved to be a student. I believe if you review and more importantly practice the strategies in this book, you will naturally begin to sprinkle mindful moments into your classroom. It is not until you experience the benefits yourself that you will truly find value and a reason to do so.

By my third visit to a fifth grade classroom I felt a wonderful shift in the students' awareness. My visits were brief (thirty minutes max, once a week), and my intention was not only to teach mindfulness but to support the teacher through my own mindful observations. Although numerous behaviors and concerns had been brought to my attention, I knew my personal agenda could potentially sabotage student progress. Therefore, while I was with the students I had no agenda. I would tell the students there are no timelines to understanding mindfulness. If you understand today, great, if it takes you until the end of the year, that is great too. Students are unused to a lack of agenda. However, through elimination of agenda, the students suddenly became more open and willing to try what I had to offer. How did I know? They began to ask questions. I no longer had to feed them the information instead they became hungry for it.

TRY THIS!

Talk about the yellow light. Students understand that a green light means go and red light means stop. What about the yellow light? The yellow light is equally important as it teaches students how to yield. By encouraging your students to pause and check in with their breathing you are promoting an attitude of yielding. It is ingrained in our culture that effort is everything. What about the value of non-effort? Non-effort is associated with not doing anything. However, when applied consciously non-effort is a valuable means for checking in with the self before moving forward.

Mindful observations are a tool for bringing self-awareness into action. They support your guide foundation by allowing you to model and experience self-awareness. Your self-awareness tones down reactivity, broadening your choices for how to respond to the needs of your students. Mindful observations promote an environment of security through feeling what is yours. Even if your feelings are triggered by someone else they are still your feelings. This type of environment produces comfort in being who you are while simultaneously encouraging positive risk taking, strength, and a thirst for learning.

When practiced regularly, at least once daily, mindful observations deepen your ability to reflect on your teaching. These self-reflections loosen patterns or ways of responding that may no longer serve you or your students well. In the next section learn how self-reflection reveals itself and how this insight sharpens your ability to communicate with students.

Self-reflection is a way of seeing yourself. As you observe yourself in front of your students, you may be witnessing a reproduction of what you feel. If you see students scattered or out of sorts consider tuning into your inner environment. Ask yourself do I feel disjointed? When you ignore or disconnect present experiences from bodily responses your students become something to manage as opposed to sources for insight. In this section these responses are referred to as hidden messages, the spoken, and unspoken messages in your classroom. When left untouched these messages suppress self-reflection and may deflate potential power.

HIDDEN MESSAGES

Hidden messages are *indirect* forms of verbal and non-verbal communication. They are often learned through families, friends, previous teachers, the school culture, or society at large. When a teacher sits in a meeting choosing to keep quiet rather than speak about what is really on her mind she may be responding to a hidden message. Perhaps it is a message from society that women should be more passive or a school culture message that teachers should be careful about what they say in meetings. Perhaps a teacher doesn't want to speak out as it will impact the work load of another teacher. Hidden messages also surface in classroom settings. Verbal comments such as, if you have nothing nice to say, don't say it at all offer a different meaning than, be respectful. The hidden message behind the former may be don't talk about your feelings, be nice, or pretend you're fine. Words and non-verbal body language are more likely to convey hidden messages when awareness is dulled. They seep into language through quick responses that may function as barriers to the present moment. Their consequences are apparent in decreased risk taking, stifled communication, and weaken self-esteem. The more aware you are, the more consciously you communicate. Messages transform into healthy communication through practice, clarity, and awareness.

Awareness is a key contributor to communication and the development of rapport. For example, eye-rolling indicates a lack of concern or patience. Students may misinterpret non-verbal gestures that lack awareness as judgments of who they are. When insensitive or delivered with defensiveness hidden messages dismantle the development of trust. This increases the chance that students and staff may repress feelings, limit risk taking, inhibit creativity, and harbor resentments. Author, Stephen D. Brookfield, *The Skillful Teacher*, states, "Skillful teachers realize that most of their procedural decisions (what content to teach next, what examples to use to illustrate a complex idea, who to call on in discussion, how to frame an assignment, the amount of time needed for small group break-outs, when to depart from the plan for the day and so on) should be guided by an *awareness* of how students experience the classroom"(p.28). This awareness is cultivated by your observations and willingness to listen for the messages you repeat. Below are some further examples of verbal and non-verbal words and statements to be aware of in the classroom setting. Each is followed by a possible hidden message.

VERBAL	HIDDEN MESSAGE
It is no big deal.	Your feelings should not matter.
I see Jimmy is sitting nicely.	Jimmy is better you, I like him more
Boys will be boys.	Boys are supposed to act out

The other class was ready quicker. I like the other class better.

NON-VERBAL	HIDDEN MESSAGE
Sighing.	I am tired of this.
Rolling eyes.	I don't believe you.
Crossing arms.	I am angry.
Squinting eyes.	I don't trust you.
Silence. Beware.	

To deflect communicating with hidden messages try practicing mindful observations. Become interested in your bodily movements, words, phrases, or repetitive thoughts. Know your observations of bodily movements are a form of listening. Notice any tension in your lips, fingers, or eyes. Just by noticing you are increasing the chances your messages are communicated purposely and purely.

Mindful observations provide insight into potential hidden messages that may misconstrue the message you are attempting to communicate. When a teacher stands silently with his arms crossed hoping to communicate that he or she is waiting for silence students may read the teacher's body language as communicating anger. Not all students are skillful at reading body language. You are better off communicating clearly leaving little room for misinterpretation.

Try This!

Notice your facial expressions when you talk on the phone. Your tone of voice may portray hidden messages. Try talking with your eyes softened and then use the same words speaking with your eyes squinted. Notice how this alters the tone of your voice.

Silent Signals. Silent signals are a great way to non-verbally cue students drawing them inward. For example, raising your hand and turning down the lights suggests a quiet pause. Many times students identify silent signals as indicating there must be something wrong. Consider clarifying how pausing is equal to being. They will focus their attention on themselves on what they hear, smell, and the way their skin feels. When students tune into being before their surroundings they are less likely to take direction as a personal attack. Keep in mind silent signals are also a way to point yourself to the present moment.

Cast Off Your Life Preserver

Mindful observations display the difference between prevention and attention. The purpose of prevention is to prevent something from happening or escalating. A teacher may intervene when a student is at risk for developing a poor habit. Habits such as a poor pencil grip, talking out of turn, mispronunciation of words, or neglecting to read directions may be prevented through redirection or correction. Attention on the other hand, is your ability to focus on one thing at a time.

Prevention is more fixed on the future, while attention is centered on the present moment. Prevention is leading through managing, while attention is leading through experience. These differences become obscure when there is an imbalance of use when one becomes a dominant answer. The only way to know which is favored is through mindful observations. Deepak Chopra states: "Every cell is made up of two invisible ingredients:

awareness and energy."Mindful observations provide deep insight into how your attention is distributed. To create clarity ask yourself, what is your intention? Are you trying to prevent or stop something from happening or are you being attentive to what is happening? If you find yourself wrapped up in the future or wanting things to go a certain way you may be weighted in prevention. This may contribute to mental and physical imbalances often described as stress. The effort it takes to stop or control behavior is exhausting. This makes you more susceptible to choosing ways of responding that are insubstantial simply due to the fact that you are tired and perhaps overwhelmed. Overtime rote choices may evolve into habitual patterns such as: noticing what is wrong before noticing what is right, speaking before listening, telling before asking, yelling, and thinking before breathing.

Mindful observations provide balance to the usage of prevention and attention responses. At the end of the day ponder, what you noticed most. If your recollections are predominately about what went wrong or what you did not do enough of consider sifting through your toolbox and pulling strategies that balance prevention and attention.

Try This!

Transform patrolling into connection. When students are watched solely for the purpose of preventing a problem, little room is left for connection. Connection is a blend of prevention *and* attention. The moment you find yourself searching for a problem try smiling instead. Inhale and exhale through the corners of your mouth. Notice how patrolling converts into connection.

Tension Matters

Tension is created by a force of pressure. The strain of meeting the needs and expectations of others takes its toll on all teachers. How you respond may influence the intensity, rate, and frequency of this force. Symptoms such as neck strain, back pain, and emotional discomfort such as feeling overwhelmed or isolated tend to exacerbate with tension. This may directly impact classroom experiences. Take a look at the example below:

Johnny's voice became louder as classmates encouraged him with whispers of attention. He was making his mouth sound like a musical instrument. This would have been fine if it was recess but at the time the children were split in separate reading groups. Ms. Jones felt pressure to get in some quality reading instruction since Spring break was around the corner. Immediately, she looked up from the student she was working with and stared at Johnny. Or should I say glared. Her eyes were wide and if they could speak they would have said, I am warning you. The children surrounding Johnny whispered "The teacher just saw you, you're in trouble." Johnny pretended he was reading and raised his hand to his mouth for one final sound. That was it, Ms. Jones had enough. With tension in her body, she walked swiftly with stiff arms. Her head protruded in front of her shoulders while her voice commanded, "That is inappropriate behavior and you just lost your recess young man."

The above example illustrates how classroom behavior may lead to unwanted tension. The relationship between tension in your body and how you respond to the present moment is strong. Certainly, there are times when quick reactions are warranted. For example, when you are driving a car, sharp reflexes, and swift responses are crucial. However, being able to distinguish which moments benefit from drawing inward first is beneficial. Had the teacher noticed some of her earlier bodily responses before she charged across the room she might have handled the behavior with less intensity. Perhaps if she noticed her eyes widening and scanning the room she could have watched herself moving into fight or flight mode. To circumvent this she might image exhaling through her eyes. This diffuses reactivity allowing the teacher to approach the student consciously rather than abruptly. Tension tamers such as: opening and closing your jaw, stretching your fingers and exhaling lowers tension, and increases attention.

Mindful observations diminish intensity between individuals. Reactivity moves into discipline when situations are approached calmly and respectfully. Relationships remain tied together while chains of behaviors are intersected. Emotions are then able to move freely. This reduces the likelihood of unfinished emotions carrying over into other situations.

Tension is a gift if you choose to see it that way. It allows you to find another way to be in the moment. When tension is high and awareness is low emotional energy becomes congested. This congestion contributes to low level emotions such as fear. Fear paralyzes inner movement in some cases numbing the mind and body. Actions may become robotic or automatic. Functioning off low energy leads to motions that deplete who you are. Mindful observations steer you to the inner vibrations of higher mind.

Try This!

Pay attention to your tension. When tension directs your responses try stretching and straightening your arms out in front of you. Interlace your hands and press out your palms so your fingers and wrists are able to stretch. Hold for three breaths. Now stretch your arms up overhead. Inhale as you raise your arms and exhale pressing belly toward spine as you lower them down. Hold for three breaths. This exercise can be done sitting or standing. Watch how it breaks up thinking stimulates blood flow and eases tension.

CHAPTER 5

Dissecting the Onion of Behavior

T HE ANATOMY OF BEHAVIOR IS similar to the layers of an onion's skin. The outer layer, the one most observable by others comprises chosen behavior in a certain situation or circumstance for example, a student choosing talking over listening. The next layer is coated with perception, intertwined with assumption such as a student thinking: *You don't like me.* Further peeling reveals emotion communicated through sensations, such as a student's heart pumping, jaw clenching, or the butterflies in his stomach. Expecting uniformity only brings disappointment. Refreshing your perceptions is like washing an onion. It is a way to prepare yourself from the inside out to work with behavior in a way that benefits both you and your students.

This chapter dissects the onion of behavior analyzing both behavioral fuels and influences and the improving influence of self-support upon student behavior. The purpose of the dissection is not to pick apart but rather to study each piece closely to ascertain how each one relates to the bigger picture. The big picture is the view from your heart and mind showing how everything and everyone is connected. Unhelpful comparisons are put to rest, including: us versus them, more versus less, good versus bad. These subside as cause and effect become one.

I have chosen to treat this chapter similarly to how you would approach a behavior. Rather than discussing every possible way you influence behavior I focus on a handful of ways. My hope is that you are able to take this information and apply it freely to many areas of your teaching. Everything in this chapter is in addition to what is already working for you. By no means is it meant to replace or discount any current systems you have in place. Please read this chapter in order. Digest it slowly taking in one spoonful at a time. Watch how it is all connected. Specific actions for supporting healthy behavior, what to do in the heat of it all, working with rhythm, moving through power struggles, the value of transitions are additional topics covered in this chapter.

THE INFLUENCES ON BEHAVIOR

Brain research has a great influence on the world of education. Scientists are continuously providing information to support teaching and better understand how children learn. Researcher and author Lise Eliot encourages parents and teachers to take caution with information that presents solely from the male/female brain perspective. Over focusing on how males and females differ may lead to responses that do more harm than good. Eliot states: "the male-female differences that have the most impact cognitive skills, such as speaking, reading, math, and mechanical ability, and interpersonal skills, such as aggression, empathy, risk taking, and competitiveness-are heavily shaped by learning."(*Pink Brain, Blue Brain* pp.6,7). She points out that response to males influences the behavior of females, response to females influences the behavior of males. The next section illustrates how.

STEREOTYPES

Citing differences between males and females may induce or reinforce stereotypes. Stereotypes are ways of labeling, grouping characteristics according to gender, nationality, or socio-economic group. Repeating statements such as boys are more active or girls are more emotional may at the time seem harmless but in the long run have proven to negatively influence behavior and learning. SAT scores is one area where this has occurred. Since the 1980s researchers have compared the results between genders generating much controversy over the reasons why girls in the past, have scored lower than boys in the math and science areas. One thing most researchers agree upon is the possibility that expectations lead to stereotypes. Stereotypes are belief systems that impact effort, expectations, attitude, and behavioral responses. If girls *believe* boys are more athletic or better at math they will behave in ways that live up to these stereotypes.

Boy girl comparisons may also affect parenting. In an article from the New York Times titled, *Should the World of Toys Be Gender-Free?* Peggy Orenstein reported the findings of a study of more than five thousand three year olds. The study found, "girls with older brothers had stronger spatial skills than both girls and boys with older sisters" (online 12/29/11/ pg. 2). Girls with older brothers were more exposed to visual spatial skills and visual motor experiences, such as playing with blocks, Legos and puzzles. By separating toys, experiences, and attitudes into male, female categories, the big picture is compromised. Girls are more likely to try to fit in to society's judgment of girls based on beauty and sex appeal. Boys may try to fit into the boy code of being tough and less emotional. Eliot sheds light on how schools structured by test driven agendas are leading to stereotyping boys as disruptive and overactive (pg. 159). As a result, a students view of meeting expectation may be equivalent to a sense of belonging.

THE BIG PICTURE

By becoming conscious of expectations and using gender free language teachers can support the big picture allowing students to grow from who they are instead what society expects them to be. In many cases it does not matter how students are the same or different. What counts most is their experience with who they are. You can learn a lot about yourself by listening to your choice of words. Judgments, expectations, and stereotypes contain features of non-presence. Careless comments such as the ones listed below, rarely originate from the moment. If you catch yourself using such statements refrain from judging yourself. Inattentive remarks are simply a reminder to persuade yourself back to the present moment. When non-reflective statements roll off your tongue, tune into your sensations. Allow your breath to ease you into feeling the trail of sensations behind your words.

If you hear someone else use one of these statements, such as a staff member or a parent consider responding in the same way. Notice the movement behind the words as if it were your own feeling (which it actually is) and allow yourself to notice the impact of sensation. When something does not feel right inside, sensations may feel sticky almost as if they are stuck to your body as a spray lotion. Correcting the other person is a form of judgment. By feeling your sensations completely you lead by example showing instead of telling people who you are as opposed to how you would like to be seen.

Stereotypical Statements

> » Boys will be boys.

> » You throw like a girl.

> » Boys line up here, girls line up there.

> » Let the girls have a turn.

> » Boys tend to let things go more easily.

> » Boys are easier to raise.

> » Girls are easier to raise.

> » Boy girl boy girl seating.

> » Girls are so dramatic.

> » Boys don't cry.

> » Girls are hormonal.

> » Girls are emotional.

> » Boys tend to be better at math, and science.

> » Well, you know he is a boy.

By loosening your grip on predetermined labels or expectations choosing instead to feel your feelings you allow your greatness as well as the greatness of your students to shine through. Labels and expectations share a common thread of resisting growth. They keep you and your students fixated on the future or locked into thinking about the past. To loosen the grip of labels, try approaching your teaching with a sense of wonder. Treat each day as if it were the first time you met your students. Become curious about different seating arrangements, play with your use of words, and watch your students through neutral eyes. Expectations, stereotypes, and labels survive with the belief that everything is the same. Treat your students as if they are never the same person. See them as ever changing and watch old forms of thinking conscious as well as subconscious melt away.

TRY THIS!

Watch yourself. Notice how you speak to girls versus boys. Include tone of voice, frequency and comments. Do you have the same expectations for boys as you do for girls? Listen to yourself when you provide feedback. When evaluating work do you predominately comment on content, artistic ability, neatness, or punctuality? Do they vary according to gender or ability? Are you less likely to give criticism to girls or boys? If a group of boys and girls are being noisy notice who you tend to speak to first.

Recycle Your Expectations. Loosen expectations and judgments by recycling them into playfulness and curiosity. Expectations tend to focus on what you want to see in the future. Curiosity and playfulness come from a sense of wonder in the now. Rather than focusing on what you expect from others notice what you anticipate in yourself. If you expect yourself to connect with students, you might create a more flexible mind driven by curiosity about making this connection. Below are some examples:

Expectation

> » I want kids to listen.

» The students should do their homework.

Wonder

» I am curious to see how students will respond if I listen more.

» Today I am playing with a new homework assignment.

TRY THIS!

Intentional Titles. Notice when labels are used loosely to refer to students or rooms in the building. Some examples may be: the special needs room, the behavioral room, the IEP (individual education plan) kids, the gifted kids. Consider coming up with intentional titles that offer you more than location or topic. Ones that are non-gender specific are preferable. Titles that are playful, creative, historical, resource, or musical carry a different tone than SPED room.

SENSE OF BELONGING

Cultivating a sense of belonging in the classroom setting is one of the ultimate ways to influence behavior. An atmosphere of unity discourages division between students which carry feelings of loneliness or separation. Students who believe they have a purpose in your classroom focus more easily on utilizing their true potential.

You are in an ideal position to create an atmosphere where students are rightfully accepted. People typically associate fitting in with their similarities. For example, by reading a book out loud to your students you create a space where students may relate to the characters in the book or to the responses of their classmates. The act of creating a space for conversation, reflection, and open mindedness sets the tone for connection. By leading students into the present moment, you are helping students to align their unconscious and conscious minds. This is powerful as many behaviors may be unconsciously driven. Aligning the two, helps students to recognize how they respond to the world around them.

Teachers who see their students for perhaps fifty minutes weekly may feel at a disadvantage for creating comfort. Take a moment and think about a time you connected to others. Perhaps it is in a restaurant where the staff knew your name and what you like to eat or drink. All students want to know if they are noticed, heard, or liked. They need safety to be themselves, to relate to the current moment.

Creating a sense of belonging is most effective when it is delivered authentically with no agenda. Pretend your principal asked you to create a morning meeting with your students to reinforce bonding and appropriate social skills. Imagine you felt rather annoyed by this request but did not want to compromise your job so you went along with it. Students sense when intentions are out of alignment with actions, through your tone, body language, and rushed energy. Although I am a huge fan of morning meetings, an approach developed by Responsive Classroom a school wide approach to discipline and behavior. I don't believe any formal curriculum can replace the value of human connection. Anyone can foster a sense of belonging through eye-contact, a smile, active listening (chapter 2), greetings, calling students by name, sharing stories, inviting stories, asking students about their passions, special greetings, and holding the space for social relatedness.

Students may also feel a sense of relatedness through outside experiences such as sports, activities, family time, or engagement with peers. Teachers support these experiences by being mindful about the workload of their students. Students inundated with homework may have little time for friendships, family, and personal development. Do this by checking in with students, parents, and other teachers also servicing the student. I once visited a school that had a board posted in the hallway so all students and teachers could view homework assignments and upcoming tests. Anu Partanen is a writer and journalist based in New York City. She writes about Finland and its educational system. "Finland's national education system has been receiving praise because in recent years Finnish students have been turning in some of the highest test scores in the world." Partanen discusses how Finland does not have private schools and "assign less homework, and engage children in more creative play." Play is one of the most natural ways to help students feel kinship.

Generating a sense of belonging supports positive social skills and group awareness. Gathering your students in a circle elevates a community of consciousness. Those who may be struggling with the moment are lifted by the consciousness of others. The simple notion of validating your students and their presence has the potential to help them *become* an inspiration for others. When staff or parents report positive observations about a shared student take a moment and reflect on how you may have played a role in that process.

Try This!

View the classroom through your students' eyes. Imagine you are one of your students. Walk into the classroom. Ask yourself what do you see, how do you feel, how might you relate to the space? How do you belong in the classroom? What messages are portrayed?

Assign homework that promotes bonding. Some examples:

> » Have students spend time getting to know their family history.

> » Ask students to interview a family member or friend.

> » Ask parents and children play a math game, draw, or read together.

Witness how your students are resourceful. Ask yourself questions such as: What choices are they making, did they problem solve, or how did their own frustration serve them well?

How to Grow a Behavioral Onion

Learning how you may stimulate behavior requires a deeper understanding of who you are. As you allow yourself to look at your attitude, mood, stress, and reactivity your doorway to perception widens. You find freedom from duplicating responses that are a disservice to your greater good. Anything that does not serve you well most likely does not serve your students well. The most attentive responses benefit everyone. That is the bigger picture. Each area is covered in the next section along with mindful approaches for handling classroom stimulation.

ATTITUDE

Your attitude typically reflects how you feel about something or someone. It often reveals sensitive information about behaviors that may trigger your reactivity. Reactivity is similar to pouring fuel on a fire. It exacerbates behavior. A trigger feels much like a pull, an urge to do something right away, make demands, control, or stop what is happening. Triggers are usually accompanied by physical symptoms such as increased heart rate, tension, discomfort, whining, or distractibility.

In the classroom setting, if you feel the onset of physical symptoms or an emotional pull toward reactivity you can assure yourself that your attitude is reflecting something your care about. It makes sense that you want to protect it. Watch how this plays out in the example below.

> *Two middle school girls were discussing their teacher's personality. On that particular day they were commenting on how the teacher was nicer because everyone did their homework. One of the girls stated: "I hope no one screws up again so she doesn't go back to being mean." I asked these girls what their teacher did when students did not hand in their homework. They replied, "She mutters under her breath, get's snappy, and yells at the class."*

I have found in my work with middle school girls that lecturing, reprimanding, or over explaining may be interpreted as yelling. When yelling the teacher may have been subconsciously protecting something she feels strongly about. It does not matter whether the teacher feels strongly or the school is serious about homework. More important, is the teacher's ability to make the correlation between protecting and a state of non-feeling. Whenever you find yourself shielding yourself from feeling, pause, and tell yourself, this is clearly something I care about let me feel it deeply so I can respond well. Once the sensations are noticed *and* experienced reactivity deflates itself. In this example the following responses may have been effective:

» Requesting a parent meeting, including the student, to discuss the importance of homework.

» Speak to students privately and brainstorm solutions for handing in homework.

» Change or modify homework to create interest. Homework can feel much like driving the same route to work every morning. After awhile, it becomes robotic. Case in point: My daughter's favorite homework assignment was to write about what she would do with a million dollars.

Try This!

Feel rather than shield. Write down a list of the things you care about deeply in your classroom. Be honest. Think of punctuality, respect, progress, and effort. Consider these to be some of your triggers. Next time you are triggered choose to feel rather than defend your position. By doing so you are shaping your attitude to respond in a way that is empowering to both you and the student.

Visualize what an open heart looks like. Images such as: a flower opening its petals or a gate opening up to a beautiful garden. Tending to your heart in this way strengthens your connection to your heart, leaving you with a more resourceful experience than self protection.

Mood

Mood states are often confusing and frustrating at the same time. Unlike your attitude, which is more specific to how you feel about something or someone, mood resembles being stuck in one emotional state. I am sure you have heard people say, I am in a bad mood or I am in a silly mood today. Learning how to unglue yourself from mood states takes practice but the effort is well worth it as mood may rouse negative behavior.

Your students particularly those with sensitive temperaments, are very receptive to your moods. Without you realizing it they may partake in the experience of your current state (see emotions are contagious, chapter 1). You may feel, bad, or guilty about this. However, I would caution you that feeling bad or guilty is neither helpful to you or your students. Forcing or pushing your mood state aside often builds inner resistance. Choosing to meet your mood where it is through self observation is a way to honor it. Let's take the above example of the teacher muttering under her breath when students did not hand in their homework. Through self-observation the teacher notices tension in her jaw, eyes, and face. She notices she is handling her materials abruptly flipping through her book quickly. Her eyes are scanning the room for misbehavior. By noticing all of this information about herself she is valuing her emotions. Respecting mood states in the present moment allows them to move smoothly.

The examples below are listed into two groups. The first includes reactions from mood and the second responses from noticing mood. Notice the differences in the actions are based solely on awareness.

Reactions from Mood

> » Speaking out loud to a student in front of others.

> » Giving unexpected, abrupt consequences that resemble punishment.

> » Threatening to remove recess.

> » Interrupting students during questions and comments.

> » Complaining about student behavior out loud in front of others.

> » Using comparisons to others as a way to motivate others to behave.

> » Saying, "I am not in the mood."

Responses When You Notice Mood.

> » You take an inhale.

» Mindfully sip water.

» Replace thoughts such as, *how can I deal with my or others moods* to *this is an opportunity to learn and grow.*

» You take time to think about decisions and logical consequences.

» You find ways to create space for potential shifts. For example, ask students to clean out their desks.

» You open a window or take your class outside for fresh air.

» Make time for laughter, read a funny joke, or purposefully choose articles to share for the times you may need a boost of laughter.

» Smile big, picture your thoughts as a sign on a long country road. There are miles between one sign and the next. See and feel the distance between your thoughts.

Karen taught third grade. Several days in a row Karen noticed she was in a bad mood. Her students were nudging each other, treating each other poorly and complaining more frequently. It was the end of the year and Karen realized she had yet to use a personal day. She took a day off so that she could truly attend to her own feelings and needs. She used the time to take a long walk and sit quietly in silence. She allowed herself to fully experience her feelings. The next day she returned to class her emotions were clearly flowing. She felt more positive, rejuvenated, and proud that she had chosen to treat herself well. The students also benefited from the brief separation as they appeared less interested in their behaviors and more interested in what the teacher had planned for that day.

TRY THIS!

Substitute tight for tense. If your mood is agitated rather than thoughts such as, *I feel stressed*, pay attention to where the tightness in your body may be. Go to your known tight spots and acknowledge them. For example, by pressing the heel of your foot onto the floor while flexing, and spreading your toes toward your body, you may feel your tight calf muscles. Or take your ear, toward your shoulder to feel for any tightness in the neck. Your choice to experience your tightness will naturally escort you to the present moment.

Mood Mystery. Treat your mood states as if they are clues to a mystery. Your responses toward your students are evidence of ignoring possible tight spots. When left unrecognized these areas may hinder your experience with present feelings. Watch yourself closely and transform reactive behaviors into useful responses.

CLASSROOM THEATER: PERFORMING FOR AN AUDIENCE

Being an educator is much like being a performer. The students' and staff represent your audience. Each classroom recreates a new setting. Similar to a theater, there are themes, plots, moments of anticipation, suspense, and resolution. Having a classroom as an audience may pose a challenge as the behavior of your students may charge the misbehavior of others. Perhaps one student is giggling and before you know it snickers are filling the room. Student stares, whispers, and comments may travel like a virus. Similar to a comedian who seeks the reinforcement of laughter a classroom audience inadvertently reinforces student and teacher behavior.

> *Simon Cowell one of the orchestrators behind the television show American Idol left the show only to start a new reality series called the X Factor. Both shows were similar in that they strove to find star qualities in everyday talented people. The first airing of the X Factor an older gentleman came out to sing. At first it appeared that the judges were not thrilled with the performance. The audience*

soon kicked in cheering and clapping. Based on the audiences'
response, the judges soon changed their minds. Simon remarked
that this is why he created a show from the beginning with a live
audience. He wanted to include the power of the audience.

Your students, co-workers and the parents of your students are your
audience. When you speak about students or to students in front of others
you may be putting unnecessary pressure on yourself. The time to have
a discussion or report about a student is rarely in front of the audience.
Ideally, conversations with other adults and students are best conducted
in a semi-private space such as an office, teacher's lounge, or quiet corner
of the school library. I say semi-private as I do not recommend ever being
completely alone with a student or adult where no one else can view what is
going on. If conversations have to take place immediately, a quiet, and brief
conversation in the hall may be appropriate.

Viewing your classroom as an audience reminds you to slow down,
listen, and watch yourself before you speak. Audience responses may add
unwanted attention to any behavioral experience. Speaking privately with
others, creating spaces for open communication, developing non-verbal
signals, making appointments to talk, or seating students you check in with
frequently closest to you, tone down audience participation.

Try This!

Feel your concern. Very often when a teacher stops to speak to a student
in the hall, they may be concerned that the remaining classmates may get
off task, stop working or goof around. These thoughts divide your attention.
Feeling your concerns rather than thinking them is a way to knit your
attention. Feel the sensations behind your thoughts. Imagine yourself
drinking the sensation like you would drink a glass of water. Do this by
taking an extended inhale while focusing on your feelings. Exhale back to
the present moment. Consider taking it one step further and allow yourself
to feel (rather than manage) the vibrations and energy coming from the
classroom.

ACTIONS: WAYS TO RESPOND

Actions are the ways in which you choose to respond to behavior. Active responses are ones that require you to do or say something. Giving a student a logical consequence for misbehavior would be an example of an active response. Passive responses require less doing and more allowing. They are less apparent to the observer but equally effective. They include allowing a natural consequence to play out on its own without interruption. Passive responses are not to be confused with laid back or limited effort. Both active and passive responses are applied with consciousness. With passive responses the teacher does not specifically tell or ask the student to do anything. Instead, the teacher creates perceptual space so the natural laws of cause and effect play out on their own. Examples of passive responses are connection, working with rhythm, listening, responding to your own needs, and widening your view of power struggles. In most cases, as in healthy partnerships, active and passive responses work together. The examples below illustrate this further:

LOGICAL CONSEQUENCE

Logical consequences teach and reinforce behaviors that support student growth. They are logical in how they relate to behavior, anticipated, delivered respectfully, and are realistic. Logical consequences separate the deed from the doer. They come from the mindset that the student made a mistake rather than that they *are* the mistake. They differ from punishment in how they teach appropriate behavior rather than attempt to make students pay for their mistakes.

The most challenging part of responding with a logical consequence is figuring out which one is appropriate. To help yourself decide, ask questions such as: what do I want to teach this student? What is my intention? How will I know when the student has acquired the new behavior? I find logical consequences work well if you want to teach responsibility and boundaries. Some examples of logical consequences are:

BEHAVIOR	LOGICAL CONSEQUENCE
Breaks pencil.	Fix or replace pencil.
Fidgets with toy.	Removal of toy.
Interrupts frequently.	Seat change, closer to teacher.
Runs up the slide repeatedly.	Restricted from the slide.
Students fooling around in line.	Teacher walks to alongside those students.
Scribbles on the desk.	Cleans the desk.
Trouble working in a group.	Seat change.

NATURAL CONSEQUENCES

Natural consequences differ from logical consequences as they happen independently in the environment. They require little adult intervention (passive) as they are often built in consequences. The teacher simply allows the student to experience without interruption. Natural consequences are great for reinforcing responsibility and life lessons. Some examples are:

BEHAVIOR	NATURAL CONSEQUENCE
Student forgets homework.	Grade naturally decreases.
Student forgets to wear sneakers for gym.	Student cannot participate.
Student forgets to close their back pack.	Student loses personal item on bus.

Logical and natural consequences are both non-reactive forms of discipline that teach and reinforce positive behavior. They are a blend of both passive and active responses which can be an effective means for teaching responsibility and setting boundaries.

TRY THIS!

See recess or outdoor time as a right, not a privilege. The positive impact fresh air, nature, and movement have on the brain, behavior, emotional regulation, and learning is tremendously supported by research. Just like children have the right to an education, nutrition, and proper care, they also have the right to their recess. Removal of, procrastinating or utilizing recess as a control tactic, in my opinion is a form of punishment. The pure threat of removing recess may elevate student heart rates, anxiety levels and blood pressure making it more challenging for them to learn and self-regulate their responses. The only time recess should be taken away is if the child poses a risk to himself or others.

Relax your tongue. Coming up with appropriate logical consequences that do not lead to punishment can be tricky. When this occurs, tell the student there will be a consequence but you need time to think about it. Allow yourself some time to reflect on the behavior. Breathe. Ask yourself, what do I want to teach in this situation? Refrain from mentally answering the question. Instead relax your tongue in your mouth. Allow it to fall to the floor of your mouth. This releases your jaw signal to your nervous system to tone down reactivity. Authentic answers cannot be pushed or demanded. It is when you are able to surrender into the process of creating solutions that they will surface without strain. Most likely a logical consequence will rise in your mind, if a natural consequence hasn't already.

CONNECTION

Connection is a blend of active and passive response. Active response requires you to perhaps ask questions or go out of your way to be sure your students feel noticed or cared for. As a passive response, connection allows you to relate to your students through the practice of observation and active listening. Active listening requires your full attention minus the talking. This includes your body language and eye-contact (see chapter 2). These actions work especially well with students who are disengaged or have low-self-esteem.

Imagine you needed to a find a physician who could conduct a physical exam. How might you choose which physician to see? Would you go by education, background, location, referral, or insurance? I am certain all of these factors would play into your decision making. After meeting the physician what would make you want to continue receiving treatment from him? Very often, the answer is connection. Did you feel listened to, heard? Can you trust or relate to this individual? Connection is a natural motivator to building relationships. Below are some examples of behaviors followed by a response of connection.

Behavior

- » Student has a pattern of leaving the room without asking permission.

Connection

- » Ask questions. What is on your mind?

- » What were you just doing or thinking? Tell me more...

- » What can we do to help you stay in the room longer?

Behavior

- » Student has trouble getting along with her peers.

Connection

- » Connect with support staff that can help the student.

- » Create a special way you greet or check in with this student. Connect through bonding rituals such as: high five, pat on the shoulder, good morning Susan, or a post it note.

» Look for the students strengths and find a way to tap into them (i.e., job taking care of class pet).

» Roles play ways to interact with others. Exchange roles and ask questions about how it felt to be in each role. Listen.

» Take time to observe the interactions in your classroom through a state of awareness rather than a state of reactivity (chapter 4). Notice how your awareness has the power to tone down fueled feelings between students.

Behavior

» Students are talkative during lessons.

Connection

» Ask students how they feel (as opposed to what they think) about the lessons and listen. Feelings foster connection.

» Allow students to be part of brainstorming solutions. When students are a part of the process of problem solving they are more likely to follow through.

» Provide an incentive at the end of the lesson, for example, ten minutes of free time to talk. Be sure to keep the incentive obtainable as in free talk time at the end of the lesson as opposed to the end of the week.

» When expectations lead to disconnection it indicates that you may not be meeting the students developmental level. You know students are being met at their level when they appear engaged, interested, or in some cases chose to show up.

» Celebrate your mini milestones.

» Use humor.

» Incorporate music and art into your curriculum. If you are studying Mexico, play music from that culture. Music connects students to the material and to each other.

Connection is a way to feed the student – teacher relationship. It is a response that asks you to feel and relate to your students. It works well with students who may be disengaged in the classroom setting. To maintain the authenticity of connection it is important to set your intention to connect, letting go of any ulterior motives, expectations, and agendas. Expectations in this case may hinder the process of connection.

RHYTHM PROVIDES A FREE RIDE INTO THE PRESENT MOMENT

Rhythm is the natural fluctuation of the mind and body. When rhythms are disregarded or controlled it may provoke unnecessary resistance and reactivity. For example, sounds in the room perceived as disruptions may lead to curt demands or punishments. Recognizing rhythm gives the teacher information about whether a student is attempting to self- stimulate or soothe his own inner responses. It also assists in the recognition of how you may be resisting the present moment. The present moment is far from perfect. It is rich with movement and stimulation. Educators have a choice in how they choose to view and thus experience rhythm. The examples below illustrate this further:

Increasing Rhythm

A prevention specialist whose job was to support families and teachers in the school building observed a four-and-a-half year old little girl during free play in a preschool setting. Teachers had reported this little girl as disruptive and aggressive. The specialist witnessed several exchanges with classmates as the little girl shared roles in the pretend kitchen area. These roles included: taking turns, listening, sharing ideas, and waiting for others. At the end of free play, all of the children transitioned into circle time. The little girl transitioned appropriately into the large group. She engaged in the circle like pop corn popping. With enthusiasm and excitement she participated in the singing. She made large movements with her arms and sang loudly. As circle time continued the little girl began to pop more and more with excitement. The teacher spent the majority of her time trying to tame the little girl's energy. She did this through statements like "pretzel legs, hands to self, and quiet voice." The teacher spoke softly, with little expression, or bodily movements. The teacher and the little girl were having opposite experiences. The teacher then chooses a different child to report the weather to the group. She did this by giving the other child pom poms like a cheer leader would use. The child very timid hardly raised the pom poms speaking the weather softly to the group. The little girl that this specialist had come to observe was barely able to restrain herself. She waved her arms around as if she was trying to lift the stimulation in the room as a real cheerleader would. At that moment, the specialist was able to recognize the rhythm. The little girl wanted to raise the stimulation while the teacher wanted to tone it down.

In the above example the teacher and student were in opposition. Had the teacher viewed the moment as an opportunity to blend rhythms, the teacher may have been able to preserve her own energy while meeting the needs of the little girl. Perhaps the teacher could have asked the entire group to imagine they had poms in their hands and to shake them together to support the student giving the report.

Toning Down Rhythm

Students attempting to tone down stimulation in your classroom may indicate it through self-soothing behaviors. Self-soothing behaviors such as: humming, pencil tapping, whispering to a friend, closing eyes, seat wiggling, or placing heads down on the desk may be due to overstimulation.

A five year old boy named Jack displayed a need to tone down stimulation when he randomly started to hit or call another child stupid. Jack attended pre-care, therefore his time at school was longer than the majority of his classmates. Rather than over focusing directly on the behavior (i.e., hitting and name calling) his teachers decided to focus on the stimulation. They recognized that Jack needed more opportunities for quiet time to help him sustain the length of his day. A parent volunteer or floating staff member spent twenty extra minutes with Jack each day doing a calming activity (reading, listening to a book on tape, or playing with play doh) in a quiet space. This intervention increased Jack's positive behaviors making it unnecessary for the teachers to utilize other forms of behavioral strategies.

Noticing rhythm influences behavior by supplying connection while respecting individual differences. This softens the need for you to manage behavior. Managing behavior is exhausting and at times unrealistic. Behavior is not something you fully control. However, with awareness it can be influenced. Rhythm work is about noticing the student's body and whether he or she is attempting to tone down or increase stimulation.

Imagine one or two of your students are off task. Their bodies are moving, they are looking around the room or out the window, perhaps even interrupting. By taking a moment and saying, OK class, before you begin this next problem let's all do a big stretch with our arms, shake our hands, twist and turn in our seat, you are utilizing rhythm. Encouraging movement is one of the best ways to brings students back to the moment. It trains students that what is happening inside of you is directly tied to the perceptions of what is happening outside of you. By asking them to move their bodies you are asking them to breathe. Rhythm work communicates to the students that you *are* paying attention therefore eliminating a need to act out. Incorporating rhythm into your daily experiences loosens attachments to things beyond your control. The more you practice rhythm work the easier it is to apply. In fact, once you see the benefits you may no longer wait until the behavior escalates before applying it. See it as a means of connection. You might approach a student and suggest: they get a quick drink of water, take a moment to stretch, squeeze a stress ball (for increasing stimulation), or do tapping (see **Try This!**). If you see some students looking out the window, rather than competing with what is happening outside, embrace it. You could say, Wow, everyone look at the lighting or the colors in the sky today. Or that person walking their dog is taking advantage of this wonderful day. Teachers feel torn about giving attention to anything outside the curriculum, in fear that they may lose their students attention. The reality is they may already be distracted and your attempt to manage behavior through ignoring may impose standards that teach students to hold back who they are. Instead, envelope it, incorporate it into what you are doing or use it as a teachable moment. By doing so you are modeling how noticing the simple things in life, is in fact a part of rhythm. Rhythm offers you a free ride back to the present moment.

> One evening my middle school daughter needed to study for a test. She sat at the kitchen counter attempting to memorize the countries and capitals of South America. At that moment she was doing anything but study. She tapped her pencil, looked around the room, wiggled in her seat, got a drink, and listened to other conversations. I kept redirecting her back to her paper, reminding her to get to work. This was not working. I paused and started watching her bodily movements. By simply watching my interpretation of her bodily movements shifted from seeing these movements as distraction to viewing them as rhythm. Her body was begging for movement. Rather than remind her once again, I said, "Learn it through your body.""Sing the words, dance, jump, move any way you like, and study."Within minutes, I and my three daughters were singing the capitals and countries while rhyming them to Christmas music. The singing moved into dancing and the potential moment for opposition (my judgment and her defense) transformed into a moment of connection, simply through the noticing of rhythm.

When I honored my daughter's rhythm, allowing her to study her own way, I went to bed feeling connected, confident, and proud of the choice I made. There are days when I sound like a broken record and work hard attempting to control or change the rhythms of others. Those are the days that wear me down most. Teachers know when they have called or spoken to a student too many times. All teachers have at some point gone to bed feeling worn down from the constant management of behavior. Rhythm work allows you to let go, notice the student's body rather than the behavior, and blend opposition rather than attempting control.

TRY THIS!

Tapping. Authors Pratt and Lambrou are two of many clinical psychologists who practice the ancient non-invasive technique of tapping they refer to as Emotional Self Management (ESM). ESM also referred as EFT Emotional Freedom Technique is gaining more popularity as the evidence for the benefits of this practice grow. By tapping with your fingers on specific areas of the body, teachers and students are able to respond to the language of their own rhythm. For example, if students are fidgety the tapping sequence would go as follows:

> *Tap lightly inner corners of eyebrows, then move to under the eye, under the lip, under the arm (near arm pit), and finally at the collar bone. Do this sequence several times over the course of a minute or so using both hands. As the teacher use your own body as a gauge. For example, you check in with your level of reactivity (scale of one to ten) before you tap and then after. Watch how you are able to bring yourself down a few notches. Notice any changes in your breathing, attention and overall stress levels.*

(Sequence taken from *Instant Emotional Healing*, 2006, pg.153).

EXPERIENCES OF THE INNER ONION: POWER STRUGGLES & TRANSITIONS

Power Struggles

Power struggles are high emotional reactivity driven by the desire to stop, or change what is happening in the moment. Power struggles feel like two opposing forces. Heightened emotions spark sharp demands, quick thinking, and separation. Power struggles range in duration from seconds, minutes, and hours. In some cases they thread their way through a lifetime of relationships. They are invited by stress and fueled by perception. When understood they offer insight, deep understanding, and mutual appreciation.

Learning the workings behind power struggles has many advantages. The biggest is a clearer understanding of the relationship between your emotions and behavior. Since power struggles are emotionally stimulating it seems natural to want to make them stop. It is easy to blame or project your behavior onto others as it can feel like they are the cause of your emotions. When misunderstood these feelings create symptoms of stress projecting outward through behaviors such as sharp tone of voice, glaring eyes, yelling, demanding, and abrupt movements. Tantrums, meltdowns, and resistance are some of the behaviors children exhibit when emotionally overloaded in a power struggle. Releasing the feelings that fuel power struggles such as anger and frustration provides only temporary relief. More damaging are the unconscious long-term feelings of hurt, betrayal, and weakened self-esteem.

THREE STEP PROCESS

Creating a new relationship with power struggles is a three step process. First, become less interested in labeling situations and people including yourself. Second become aware of how you invite powers struggles into your teaching. Third, honor differences by being present in your moment. Once these three steps are applied, power struggles transform into experiences of growth.

LET GO OF MY LABEL

Labels are like titles or categories that describe a student or job description. For example, a student may receive the label of Attention Deficit Disorder to receive modifications such as extra time on tests or preferential seating in the classroom. A teacher may be labeled as a special educator who is in charge of carrying out services to students who are labeled as learning disabled. For those reasons labels are beneficial and required. It is when labels are repeated either silently in your head or out loud that power struggles may surface. Labels maintain reactivity as they are often attached to thinking. When your thoughts dominate your actions your body is drained from an absence of presence.

Sam was an eleven year old boy diagnosed with Autism. Hilary was Sam's one to one aide in the classroom setting. Hilary spent most of her time with Sam helping him to integrate into the regular classroom setting. One day Sam was asked to put some items he was playing with away and he resisted by raising his voice and attempting to grab the items back. Immediately, Hilary thought to herself, I need to quiet him down, he is going to disrupt the other students. She remembered what had worked in the past when a power struggle started to emerge. She said a firm, "No" and placed the new task in front of him. This time Sam was not going to comply. Immediately, Hilary started thinking about the future. Her thoughts ranged from, I can't let him win to Maybe I better remove him from the classroom.

In the above example, Hilary took it upon herself to label herself as the fix it person. She assigned herself the title of the person who controlled or fixed Sam's inappropriate behavior. Attempting to fix another person's behavior is ultimately a dead end street. The prolonged usage of labels turns experiences into problems. Rather than having an experience with Sam, Hilary saw her situation as having a problem with Sam. Labeling her situation as a problem then led to Hilary having to *do* something about it. On the other hand, seeing her situation as an experience requires her to *be* with Sam. Both viewpoints allow Hilary to arrive at the same destination. The first does it through draining Hilary by inducing her body into a stress response (I must do something quickly) the second feeds Hilary strength, and clarity by allowing her to be present in the experience.

TRY THIS!

Surrender Labels. Reflect on how you define your role as an educator. Ask yourself, who am I? Hear the answer. Ask yourself again, who am I? Hear the answer. Keeping asking and listening to your responses. Try not to judge or analyze what you say to yourself. Notice the labels you may place unknowingly on yourself (I am a counselor, I am a teacher, I am a mother, I am a nurse). Treat this exercise as an experience in itself.

How Power Struggles are Invited Into Your Classroom

Power struggles are invited into your teaching through stress and expectation. When your stress is high, the number of your thoughts increases. Over thinking may lead to unnecessary confusion, panic, and frustration. A young child may cry because they think you are going to put them in time out. An older student may become inflexible or frustrated because they think they will not be able to meet your expectations. When your thoughts dominate your feelings it may trigger behaviors in you such as: talking too much, over explaining, lecturing, inflexibility, over sensitivity, and poor communication. All of which move you away from the present moment, inflaming possible power struggles.

How Mini Moments Prepare you for Macro Moments

In the heat of the moment, you can reach into your tool box and come up with a handful of strategies that will in fact deescalate the heat of a power struggle. However, a long term approach to working with power struggles is through the development of consciousness. In this case, it means spending time getting to know your less intense reactions. Your less intense reactions are what I refer to as the mini moments of your day. Perhaps the photo copy machine gets jammed with paper or a student arrives late to class. Take these mini moments and utilize them as opportunities to practice experiencing rather than reacting to what is happening. Mini moments familiarize you with sensations that are less emotionally charged. Later when you are in the midst of a power struggle your bodily reactions will not seem so overwhelming. This familiarity encourages responsiveness and confidence rather than reactivity.

> *Kathy, a tenth grade teacher decided to practice being in her mini moment each time she went to the copy room to retrieve her mail. She would notice herself sort through her mail. She would notice the size of the envelopes, handwriting, weight, and how the paper felt in her fingers. Within seconds Kathy felt more grounded in the*

present moment. Retrieving her mail in this way allowed Kathy to feel focused and less overwhelmed by requests that may have formally triggered stress in her.

Try This!

Sit with Tension. By sitting with your tension you are choosing to *be* with your tension rather than react to it. Notice your tension, where it rests in your body, and then feel it through. You can sit with tension while listening to phone messages, making copies, before you press the send button on your e-mail, and after looking at the clock.

Empower the situation. Any time you offer choices you honor yourself and the student. As the teacher you have the privilege of selecting which choices are available. The student has the privilege of choosing the one that works for him. With younger children it is best to keep the choices to a minimum of two or three: you may draw or read.

Clarify. Anytime you clarify what you say or what you hear, you empower both yourself and the student. Avoid code language, making assumptions, or telling students what they should do. Should or have to language may hold people back from their true potential. Instead state, I would like you to or it is important to. Be sure to clarify homework assignments or instructions with brief, clear language. Notice if you use your tone of voice as a way to exert power in a I told you kind of tone. Also watch your tone at the end of a sentence. If your voice goes up you may be confusing a question with a statement? Ask questions such as, would you like another example?

Transitions

Transitions are the spaces between moments. During the school day they are often viewed as the movement from one activity to the next. They tend to be measured by their level of disruption. For instance, transitioning students from the task of reading to writing may require less mental and physical energy then transporting students from reading to lunch. This section illustrates the value of viewing transitions as opportunities to create internal shifts. Internal shifts travel cellularly creating biochemical changes that promote alertness from energy rather than from fear.

In the book *Transitions: Making Sense of Life's Changes* by William Bridges, the author discusses how society "confuses the words change and transitions." He describes change as situational and transition as psychological. Teachers may be trained (by themselves as well as others) to view transition as a spring for potential problems or stress. For example, with the growing awareness around bullying teachers are expected to supervise student behavior during unstructured times such as dismissal or lunch. Expecting problems may elevate stress hormones such as cortisol, wrecking havoc on the body as the hormones responsible for cellular repair are obstructed. It is not only possible but in some cases critical for teachers to learn how to monitor students without sending signals of threat or danger to their nervous systems.

Transitions are not just about getting you ready for the next experience, they *are* the experience. Learning how to focus on the in-between times with consciousness is key to creating new neurological pathways that support overall health. To support this trend, health must become your wealth. Your well-being is based on more than what you eat or the amount of exercise you do. It is a commitment to a mindset of noticing how your thoughts impact your beliefs and decisions. If you desire higher test scores, academic achievement, or students that transition well, health must become the gateway to these fortunes. In this case it is the abundance of your sensations and how they aid your effectiveness with transitions.

Transitions are similar to the fluctuation of thoughts in the mind. Some thoughts move in and out smoothly, while others stick or become pronounced. Teachers are masters at picking up behavioral patterns such as talkative or active that occurs during certain times of the year such as the holidays. This may spike anger and frustration as rules and expectations previously laid out need to be revisited. You may hear yourself or other staff members reiterating the rules as they move through hallways. Your approach to working with transitions needn't change. By focusing your attention on your present emotional energy, (your wealth), situations you encounter flow more easily as the changing of the tides. Transitions also change form and consistency. Healthy responses, ones that promote respect, individuality, and non-assumptive thinking support the natural flow of all transitions. In a state of flow non-reactivity and acceptances are fruitful.

> *Twice a week Kelly monitored lunch. She watched students as they traveled to lunch and purchased their food, interacting with students, cleaning up, and lining up. The majority of her time she spent reinforcing the rules, reminding students to be quiet, settle down, walk, or raise their hands. When possible she would attempt to interact with students by asking questions or engage in side talk. However, most often her energy was split between engaging and keeping things under control.*

The challenge of assigning yourself the role of a referee is taking on the added responsibility of directing the behavior of others. In other words, students are likely to do what you say to keep you calm and happy. You as opposed to your students' awareness become a barometer for good or acceptable behavior.

Transforming Transitions Into Moments of Acceptance

Transforming transitions into moments of acceptance allows you to see and experience the benefits transitions have to offer. Some of these benefits include: human connection, self-care, and movement. Cultivating acceptance is very different than cultivating approval. By keenly drawing your attention into the present moment you are connecting to acceptance. Acceptance is different than dwelling. Dwelling feels like a preoccupation with thoughts or an attachment to a way of responding such as a habit of telling students to be quiet. To activate acceptance apply the following three steps:

1. See transitions as opportunities to pay attention to your inner needs. For example, are you thirsty? Do you need a bathroom break? Time alone or time with others?

2. Keen in the moment by setting the intention of acceptance. You are not trying to change, get rid of, or stop this moment but simply accepting it as it is. Notice your moment without judgment. Do this by allowing yourself to pay attention to

subtle awareness's such as the color of the foods on your plate. By noticing what is on your plate without judgment, you are accepting what is on your plate.

3. Watch how a state of acceptance alters your responses toward yourself as well as your students. For example, tapping a student on the shoulder instead of yelling across the room.

In 2009 Timothy J. Fox conducted an extensive research project, *Effective Transition Techniques.* His research was based on daily transitions that took place in a sixth grade classroom in Portland, Oregon. His focus was to uncover some of the best practices for transitioning students safely and promptly in order to preserve more time for classroom instruction. During his research he discovered a vision for transitions by B. Baker. Baker stated, "Transition time should provide children with an opportunity for continued imaginative, and creative thinking. Activities should be motivating, relaxing, and reinforcing. "Transitions should prepare children for the experience to follow" (Baker 1992, p.17). Fox's research revealed a study by Mendler and Curwin (cited by Kariuki and Davis (2000) in which it was suggested that "in order to motivate students to engage in appropriate behavior they needed to know that their efforts and actions have value. Also, students needed to feel that they were special and loved. Using a positive discipline model, Kariuki and Davis (2000) found that students were able to transition, on average, in only 41 seconds, compared to 5.6 minutes before the intervention. Students were more willing to decrease their transitions because they were **empowered** to make choices to improve their classroom environment."

When transitions are taken for granted or treated as simply a means to get from point A to point B disconnection occurs. Students and teachers may become disconnected from themselves. Quality of presence is one of the ways to keep learning alive. Consider viewing transitions as an addition to your day, rather than something that takes something away. To honor transitions means to honor the space in between tasks. By doing so you are choosing to accept and appreciate the now.

Tips for transitioning young children:

» Play Mozart. Don Campbell has conducted extensive research on the benefits of certain types of music, including classical. Some of the research reveals classical music's role in the improvement of test scores, decreases in hyperactivity, reduction of errors, and body healing.

» Ring a chime. Chimes have a tone that vibrates through the body encouraging relaxation and attention.

» Sing transition songs.

» Use an hour glass or minute glass. This provides a visual and also has a meditative quality as children are encouraged to watch the sand pouring as a gauge for time.

» Call students to line up by directing them into the moment. For example, calling students into line according to the color they are wearing encourages them to stop and pay attention to their own clothes.

» Ask students to visualize the feeling they desire during transition time. What would it feel like in their bodies to experience a transition that is peaceful, kind, and considerate to others?

» At the end of a task, give students the option of sitting still, journaling, doodling, or breathing for a minute or so before they begin the next task.

TRY THIS!

Comb your hair. This is a tool you can utilize on yourself as a way to move emotions that feel stuck or congested. Imagine the palm of your hand is a comb. Cup your palm in front of eyes as if your hand were an eye-pillow but without touching your face. While taking a long inhalation and a long exhalation move your hand slowly from the front of your forehead to the top of your head and all the way down to the nape of your neck. Do this several times while breathing. If you feel panicky, angry, or rushed imagine combing the energy of this fear through your hair beginning at the hairline and down the nape of your neck.

Unconscious stress. It is preferable to do this before you begin your day. Ask yourself why you are stressed and rate it on a scale of one to ten. Close your eyes and imagine breathing into the stress. Author Alex Loyd discusses how the sources of internal stress are often due to memories stored in the hypothalamus of the brain. When identifying internal sources of stress it is important to close your eyes and allow any visual memories to surface. For example, I had a visual memory of myself as a six year old little girl with the feeling of disgust in my heart. Closing my eyes, rating my stress, and breathing allows me to pull up these pictures and send the energy of love to these stored memories. Much of what is reacted to during the day comes from the unconscious mind.

How you perceive behaviors and the challenging moments of your day greatly influences your response. Your perception is influenced by conscious as well as unconscious thoughts, feelings, and memories. The intensity of your reactions may be a signal from within to observe pay attention to your moment as opposed to the experiences of those around you. Your experience of the present moment helps you to understand, direct, and guide your students well.

CHAPTER 6

Temperament

TEMPERAMENT IS NATURAL, MADE UP of inborn behavioral traits. These traits are biological and share the role of developing personality through life experiences. Understanding temperament is like focusing the lens on your camera. When viewed with the clear lens of your perception, the biological makeup of your students became apparent and appreciable. Understanding temperament also makes your job as a teacher easier. It gives you the freedom to let go of trying to fix, change, or control behavior. When temperament is understood, worked with, and appreciated students flourish.

This chapter identifies temperament and how to recognize it teaching you to shift from identifying temperament to complimenting it. This includes developing your teaching style through the use of a language called Heart Talk. Heart talk tones down reactivity while strengthening creative problem solving.

My daughter's preschool class walked into the classroom wearing angel robes with halo's over their heads singing Twinkle, Twinkle

Little Star. As I looked at all their lovely faces, hints of temperament traits colored the room. Some were smiling and waving to their parents others were distracted or gazed at the floor. The students were organized into a row looking directly out at the audience of parents and family members. The audience resembled the paparazzi with all the camera's and video players in action. The little girl next to my daughter stood up and crossed her arms, with a frown on her face. Her parents and teachers tried to encourage her non-verbally and she shook her head no, standing her ground. Normally, this little girl was quite friendly and interactive however; in front of an audience she showed a different trait.

Daycare providers have a brighter view of temperament as it is more clearly evinced in infancy. Once children enter school behavior is a blend of temperament, personality, learned behavior, and development. Temperament distinguishes itself as it speaks to the innate qualities of students. These innate qualities connect you to the core make up of your students. Some people may interpret the above situation as misbehavior or attention seeking behavior. I see it as temperament. You may wonder if the little girl in the above scenario will always be like this. Most likely not she will probably grow and learn how to cope with experiences that bring out her traits of shyness and persistence. For example, as a child Cindy often felt shy, so her twin brother learned to speak for her. Today, Cindy speaks in front of large groups four to five times per week. She states: "I still feel inwardly shy, I just have learned ways to cope with it." Temperament is not set in stone. The way you teach, communicate, and discipline helps students see the advantages of various temperaments.

RECOGNIZING TEMPERAMENT

Initially, you'll need some awareness of temperament traits. While most psychologists and researchers agree on the concept of temperament not all agree on the traits. The purpose of this section is to provide you with a sense of how temperament may show itself in the school environment. If you would like to know more about the specific traits researched I would suggest you refer to the bibliography section of this book. In the mean time, observing children in unfamiliar situations along with caregiver conversations offers a genuine perspective about student temperament.

I am always amazed at how unfamiliar situations highlight temperament. Observe a child approaching Santa Claus, speaking, or performing in front of a group, transitioning into a new classroom, or trying something for the first time and you see temperament. Like development, temperament comes with a range (low to high) and no student fits one specific trait. Temperament is a blend of several traits. J. Kristal provides a quick survey of a child's temperament in her book, *The Temperament Perspective*. The survey lists temperament traits and allows teachers and caregivers to rate students on a scale of one to five. These traits include: "sensitivity, activity, intensity, regularity, approach/withdrawal, adaptability, persistence, distractibility and mood" (2005, pg. 83). In the classroom setting, low persistence would be evinced by a student who could not work for long periods of time. Students with high sensitivity may become overwhelmed or upset easily in a classroom with high or prolonged stimulation. Students who are easily distracted may have difficulty in classrooms with excessive movement, noise, or a teaching style that caters toward auditory learners.

Teachers who see large groups of students once a week need to be keen observers as they have fewer opportunities to learn about their student's temperament. To observe keenly, (Chapter Four), view temperament through your heart not your head. True recognition of temperament comes from genuine interest in your student's individual identities. Learning about their innate qualities requires less talk and more observation. To achieve this, you must be fully prepared for your students your lesson plan in place, materials ready, and complete presence. When you observe your students in groups, working alone, learning, trying something new, or responding to a change you are observing temperament. You know you are observing from your heart when there is no agenda. Your heart's compassion generates an open mind permitting you to observe who your students are not just how they are performing. This may be accomplished through spontaneous observation, on a child's level perhaps observing play or an interaction between two students. This action approaches a situation with curiosity and presence.

A third grade teacher approached me excited to share the progress of one of her students. This student was diagnosed with ADHD and had a long history of impulsive and distracted behavior. This teacher came to me as a student of yoga. It was three weeks before Christmas I ask all of my students to try one minute of meditation daily. This teacher decided to extend this to her class. She had her students sit silently for one minute in the morning and one minute after lunch. After a couple of weeks she came to me excited at the progress she had seen in the student with ADHD. She reported a recent observation of her student in a class performance. The student was nervous and moving constantly. She made eye-contact and demonstrated taking a deep breath. Instantly, this student understood. He took a deep breath. The teacher as well as other observers could see the physical change in this student. Through breathing, silence, and a connection with his teacher he was able to be in his body. Through spontaneous observation and treating his behavior as temperament or inherent qualities, the teacher was able to empower the student through her heart.

Teachers working with students more frequently can gather more information about student temperament through communication with parents and caregivers. They are a reliable resource for broadening your view of what behavioral tendencies come naturally from and which ones are more environmentally influenced. Ask them open ended questions about their child such as: how do they do with new situations or respond to change. Find out about their child's activity level and what on a scale of one through five would they consider their child's levels of persistence, frustration, or impulse. Inquire about sleeping habits and qualities that have been clear since their infancy. Such open communication is a key component to matching student temperament.

Recognizing temperament calls for open communication, spontaneous observations, and an overall appreciation for inherent behavioral tendencies. Temperament reminds you to ask questions while challenging you to explore ways to meet the unique make-up of each student. The next section demonstrates how to do so.

COMPLIMENTING TEMPERAMENT

Teachers compliment temperament by rooting their teaching style in a partnership of mutual respect. Complimenting temperament means subscribing to the belief that all traits are contributions to the process of growth. Partnering with families and students will help you impart that message across. When temperament is ignored, controlled, or referenced in a negative way, it contributes to stereotyping individuals into categories of good or bad. Stereotyping behavioral traits may involuntarily handicap individuals. This is not exclusive to students. Educators also need to be mindful of labeling each other (e.g., the strict teacher) in a way that stifles perception. As teachers become more conscious of who they are (many times through how others see them) their skills for working with various temperaments expand. To be self aware is to be in a constant state of creating self.

The categorization of temperament traits does however, have its place. It is primarily a means for understanding, empathizing, and developing ways to reach your students. Once clarified, the next step is to develop a partnership. A partnership is similar to an agreement. The most important agreement you make is the one with yourself. Agree to watch yourself your words, responses, inner dialogue, and judgments. Notice how your body corresponds, your energy levels, tension, which traits you are attracted to, and which ones rub you the wrong way. Your willingness to notice *is* a way to take responsibility for your part. Healthy alliances are not built on finding what is wrong and how to fix it, but as an investment in the self, leading to the discovery of interaction in ways that are mutually beneficial. Watch yourself without judgment. Non-judgment is an essential ingredient to fostering respect. Teachers are trained to critique others and find ways for improvement. To critique is to notice. Noticing and judging are not the same. When the lines between noticing and judging are obscure unhealthy behaviors just as resistance perpetuate. When you are noticing you are observing. Judgment means to evaluation. By observing you are placing the focus on yourself, making you a resource for inspiration and growth for individual styles and temperaments.

I once observed a teacher on a field trip to a museum. The teacher asked a boy to deliver a message to another teacher. The teacher receiving the message stated out loud "Wow, thanks I can't believe he actually did what he was told."Comments such as these break agreements. They are hurtful and disrespectful, not only to your students but to you as well. They hurt your integrity and dampen your self esteem.

Complimenting temperament takes partnership and respect. Partnership means taking responsibility for your part while respecting differences. They are encouraged or discouraged by what you say and do. Listen and watch yourself. Your attitude toward temperament traits has a great deal of influence. By agreeing to notice your responses you are choosing to see things as they are, rather than how you would prefer them to be.

Heart

Your heart acts as a second brain. It allows you feel, sense, and regulate your body physically and emotionally. The unification of your mind and body harness response from the heart. Temperament responds well to conversations from the heart. Heart response inspires relatedness and rapport. This in turn promotes trust a key ingredient for social bonding.

This next section reveals your heart as a viable resource for responding to temperament. It gives you a view of when heart is working. Responding from your heart softens reactivity as it is driven by your body more so than your head. Your body opens the door for creative and encouraging responses. You no longer can take the same route of action. Heart prompts responses that operate with temperament and support your well being.

In order to respond from the heart you must first learn how to activate it. The heart is surrounded by a powerful electromagnetic field. Experiments conducted at the Heart Math Institute by Mc Craty, Trevor, and Tomasino have found evidence that the hearts electromagnetic field can transmit energy between individuals up to five feet apart. This means you communicate to and with your students through both your body and head. Heart energy tunes you into your senses and instincts; invoking compassion, empathy, understanding, inspiration, and love. These emotions trigger internal motivation, positive choice, and respect for others.

STIMULATING HEART

Your heart is a catalyst for feeling. When you play a piece of music or watch a movie that moves you emotionally you are rousing your heart. Art, music, writing, reading, physical movement, animals, pleasant memories, pictures, cooking, touch, a warm bath, or a hot cup of tea, are natural heart openers. Open hearted response is important to complimenting temperament. Teachers with students with challenging temperament traits need to make time to fortify their own hearts. Chapter nine provides you with ways to tend to the stream of your heart strength

HEART MOMENTS

Heart moments generate community and positive choices. They do this by regulating your heart rate, blood flow, oxygen levels, and the circulation of feel good hormones. When you laugh, smile, engage, give thanks, support, listen, encourage, notice, or hug your students you know you are functioning from your heart. When you see students holding hands, giggling, sharing, playing, being kind, volunteering, playing music, helping one another, you know they are in their hearts. Enrichment classes play a critical role in providing avenues where temperament can flourish. Conversely, heart moments can be defused by habitual control, worrying, labeling, stress, and rigidity.

I received a phone call from the parent of a child that no longer wanted to attend school. The parents reported the child worried excessively, to the point where she would vomit. The parents reported some strategies that worked with their daughter in previous years. However, they were told by teachers that their strategies were elementary and that was not how things were in middle school. The parents sought advice from various specialists who labeled their daughter as oppositionally defiant. This label upset the family and they felt weakened by the process. By the time their daughter came to me for support I knew part of my job was to reboot this family by connecting everyone involved to their hearts. Heart responses do not come from the perception that someone is broken or unfit. By teaching the family heart talk their perceptions shifted in a positive direction. They were able to generate and follow through with strategies that supported their daughter's temperament.

Heart Talk

Heart talk can be a form of verbal and non-verbal communication speaking from the present moment. Heart talk stems from listening and watching others from your heart. It is generated from a state of mind including emotions such as compassion, love, understanding, encouragement, passion, and inspiration. When applied regularly heart talk permeates your classroom stimulating an atmosphere of acceptance. Below are responses that come from the heart. Notice how the responses from the heart compare to the ones that come exclusively from the head. Heart responses are rooted in the present moment, while the head responses are focused or concerned with the future. Notice how heart talk is more connected to feeling, while head talk is connected to thinking. The expectations on educators push teachers to dominant their responses through thinking. By always focusing on what is next, little opportunity is left to honor temperament. Create balance by paying attention to the way you speak to the moment.

Heart Talk: Detaches you from the problem and redirects you to what is happening in the moment. Heart talk can be voiced out loud or stated silently in your head as a way to stay connected to others. The following words represent heart talk:

> Today, now, right now, in this moment, presently, I see, may I , I hear, I smell, You are, I am, you feel, I feel, I hear, I have, you have, you say, I say, I love, thank you, I forgive you, I forgive me.

Head Talk: Keeps you in the problem by focusing on the future. The following words represent head talk:

> After, afterward, later, what if, I better, I should, next, following, hurry up, never.

The young girl described above felt anxious about going to school. Her globalized anxiety left her with an experience of listlessness and frustration.

Heart talk offers a way to put things in perspective and tone down anxiety to a more manageable level. Phrases facilitating inward direction include: right now my breath is flowing, I am breathing in through my nose and out my mouth, I am feeling my shirt touch my skin, I am beginning to feel calm and I have all that I need to feel calm. Once calm it became evident that her heart was more open, as she could now see the value in her temperament traits. Sensitivity transformed into intuition and nervousness evolved into signals of growth.

The words in which you choose to describe your students temperament impact your perceptions and responses. Words carry a vibration. Aggressive or negative words have been scientifically proven to carry a lesser frequency than words that are kind or encouraging. Therefore, the vocabulary you choose to describe your students has potential to initiate change. Heart talks are words that are powered by *descriptions* rather than labels, with a higher frequency, and a connection to the moment. The left side below shows a list of temperament traits, the right side descriptions from the heart. Notice how the right side offers descriptions rooted in value. By focusing on value you are unconsciously and consciously choosing to view your students from a state of higher potential.

Sensitive	Responsive, susceptible, intuitive, bright, creative, insightful.
Procrastinate	Observer, feeler, passive.
Aggressive	Determined, bold, physical, energetic.
Angry	Likes boundaries, assertive, feel strongly,
Difficult	Assertive, boundless energy, direct, feels and see's everything.
Distracted	Thinking, preoccupied, creative, diverted, stimulated, visual.

Impulsive / Active	Creative, spontaneous, enthusiastic, coordinated.
Defiant	Assertive, protective, coping, visual, sensitive, vulnerable,
Whiny	Fatigued, stimulated.
Disruptive	Disinterested, animated, talkative, engaging, disengaging.
Anxious / Fearful	Cautious, pre-occupied, sensitive, feeler.

Labels stifle growth, movement, and limit creative problem solving. "Whenever you label something you deaden its aliveness."Steve Ross, p. 249. Heart talk is a way to connect to the deeper parts of self that reveal confidence, strength, love, and worthiness.

TRY THIS!

Write it down. Pick one of your students and begin to jot down on a piece of paper words that come to mind when describing his temperament. Try not to think too much or get caught up in neatness. Connect to your breath. Inflate your lungs while closing your eyes, taking three slow, deep breaths. Pause, open your eyes, flip the paper over, and write the list again. Notice any changes in the two lists or whether they stayed the same. If the words are the same try the exercise again with a more relaxed mind. Loosen your jaw and really allow yourself to *receive* your breath. Notice how your view of temperament is more influenced by receiving than doing.

GOODNESS OF FIT

Goodness of fit is when the temperament of the student blends well with the disposition of the teacher. For example, an anxious or sensitive temperament may be a good fit with a structured, less intense teacher. A distracted child may be a good fit with a spontaneous, structured, or animated teacher. In Kristal's book, *The Temperament Perspective: Working with Children's Behavioral Styles* (2005), the author defines "A goodness of fit" and examines how certain environments, teaching styles, communication styles, and discipline styles work for some temperaments and not others. Your students are more likely to grow and learn from positive experiences. Goodness of fit is a way to ensure a student is provided positive learning experience. Parents and previous teachers are helpful resources for connecting a student to a teacher who is a goodness of fit. In some schools parents are discouraged from requesting a particular teacher, while they are encouraged to focus on requesting specific teaching styles. I understand how requesting specific teachers may be problematic. However, it is important to encourage families to advocate for student temperament. When students land in classrooms that are not a good fit, it creates problems that may not otherwise exist. As a teacher it is important to reflect on the contents of your teaching style. Reflecting on how learning takes place in your classroom the auditory, visual, kinesthetic, cooperative, independent, projects, and seat work. I would recommend doing a self-assessment such as SAILS (Students Achieving Improved Learning Strategies, www.roanestate.edu), which allows you to calculate the amount of time you put into each area. Goodness of fit goes both ways. Dr. Wayne Dwyer said, "You get what you *are*, not what you want." Be clear who you are. Understand your teaching style, strengths, areas of interest, and which students blend well with your style. The clearer you are the more likely you will attract students that are a goodness of fit.

SUPPORTING TEACHING STYLE AND CREATIVE SPACES

Ideally, teachers are encouraged to accommodate all learners through various modalities. To do this you must recognize any imbalances in your teaching style. Reflect on which areas you are dominant and which areas could use strengthening. You may be a talkative teacher who spends a great deal of time explaining things out loud. Consider observing a teacher who is predominantly visual or kinesthetic to acquire some ideas for creating balance. I truly believe that teaching style needs to be an open, honest, conversation between teachers. It sets teachers up for disappointment when idealistic expectations are created. Even the most seasoned teachers have days where what worked in the past no longer works in the moment. Sharing stories and resources is an excellent way for teachers to support one another. One of the ways to encourage this type of working environment is to create a space where teacher's can meet confidentially to exchange information. Very often teams gather in spaces such as conference rooms that feel cool, sterile, or in some cases cluttered. Spaces that stimulate creative thinking are anything but sterile. When developing the new logo for Powered by Me, the graphic designer came to me with an idea that I loved. She stated "After you told me about the message you are trying to send, I turned on some music in my work space and the idea just came to me."Creative spaces are generated from an atmosphere of both giving and receiving. When little time or effort is put into receiving individuals may mistakenly develop the mindset that they are valued for what they can do instead of who they are. Teachers are more likely to view themselves as a good fit, when they are able to receive the benefits of the moment.

Temperament consists of inborn, biological traits, and natural behavioral tendencies. Working with temperament is less about managing and more about honoring. By doing so, you bring out the best in your students as well as yourself. Below in the (**Try This!**) section I have listed some questions to consider when creating a space where staff can both give and receive. I realize space in schools is limited and some are only available certain times of the day. I would suggest you start small perhaps beginning with a space where you hold team meetings. If you find the space is working you will naturally want to share the concept with others. For schools that may not have a conference space, you may have to begin with a section of a room, table or desk.

Try This!

Questions to consider when creating a space that stimulates creative thinking:

> » What is the true purpose of the space? On the surface it may be a place to hold meetings and private discussions. What kind

of energy do you wish to feed these conversations (acceptance, innovative, kindness)?

» If the space could speak what would it say? Perhaps may this space be a place where your creativity sparks, individuals are inspired, respected and connections grow.

» What kind of feeling do you wish to promote in the space? Choose colors that support that feeling such as yellow for energy or soft greens for calming. Consider the lighting maybe replace fluorescent lights with lamps. Ideally find a space with a window for fresh air and perhaps a plant.

» What sounds and smells might you experience in this space?

» Are there visuals that support your intention? What kind of pictures are on the wall? Consider incorporating pictures of nature or art work.

» Are you able to receive the energy behind the visuals? If a space is cluttered with visuals it may promote a feeling of overstimulation or distractibility.

CHAPTER 7

Power Tools

SELF AWARENESS IS ONE OF the essential building blocks for the development of social, emotional, and intellectual growth. Power tools are classroom strategies, implemented by the teacher, which reinforce the skills building self-awareness. Power tools must have two essential ingredients, awareness and presence. Every strategy a teacher chooses to implement can be transformed into a power tool when these two ingredients are incorporated. It is not necessary for teachers and students to maintain a state of awareness for these tools to be effective. All it takes is one individual making the conscious choice to be saturated by the moment. This choice powers the tool.

A traditional tool transforms into a power tool when educators teach social/emotional skills, such as learning to label feelings. Students learn what it looks like to be happy, sad, mad etc. When a student is able to experience sadness or anger with awareness and presence this basic teaching tool transforms into a power tool.

This chapter offers twelve power tools that promote self-awareness in the classroom setting. Applying these tools strengthens a student's ability to see how what they sense and what they feel has the ability to guide them well. As a teacher, you may find students no longer have to be busy attempting to figure out how they fit in or how they are unique. Self awareness releases any need to act out. It is the practice of valuing who you are. Self awareness is less about comparing or rating yourself against others and more about paying attention to oneself.

DEVELOPMENT OF SELF-AWARENESS

It may seem premature to think about reinforcing self-awareness in the earlier years of child development. However, research shows that human beings are born with a built in capacity for self-awareness. Researchers such as Amiel-Tison and Grenier (1980) illustrate how some of the early tactile experiences in the womb such as thumb sucking illustrate the beginnings of self-awareness. In the article, *Five levels Of Self-Awareness As They Unfold Early In Life*, author Philippe Rochat reports that "self consciousness is the ability to have others in mind when they behave and it begins around two and three years of age."(p.717-731, 2003). Strategies that promote self-awareness strengthen social skills, empathy, communication, and confidence.

WHAT'S IN THE TOOL BOX?

Many seedlings for planting self awareness have already been sprinkled throughout this book. The twelve power tools explained below are not the only means for enhancing self awareness but certainly are enough to get you started. The purpose of presenting you with these twelve tools is to open up your perception so you are able to see how you may be encouraging or discouraging self awareness in your classroom. Use this as an opportunity to strengthen your own awareness. Try not to compare or contrast what you do. This is not an assignment, nor is it meant to tell you what to do. Without your awareness, these tools will fall short. Read each section, while breathing mindfully. Notice in which ways you may relate to the material.

#1 Tool: Teach students how to Breath

When you teach students how to breathe you teach them to value who they are in the exact moment. Breathing is the quickest and most effective way to achieve *being*. When breathing, you are feeling and growing. One way to teach breathing is to relate it to a mental image or physical movement. This helps students receive benefits from breathing and visualization, a stress- reduction technique proven to lower blood pressure. On inhale, your belly blows up like a balloon, on exhale your belly deflates. Below are breathing and visualization techniques that are easy to incorporate into your classroom setting. They are written as scripts that can be read aloud word for word. Feel free to alter them for your comfort and voice.

Try This!

Scripts for teaching breathing skills:

Long Inhale, long exhale

The Flat Tire: Okay, everybody sit up tall, relax your shoulders, and take a deep inhale through your nose. Exhale through your nose. Imagine you have a flat tire on your bike and blow the tire up on inhale, puffing your belly out. Watch your belly rise and on exhale feel your belly release as if air was coming out of the tire. Keep imagining you're putting air into the tire, on inhale and taking it out of the tire on exhale. Breathe slowly keep relaxing your shoulders and face. Feel free to close your eyes.

Yawn Breath:

Everyone let out a big yawn. Open your mouth wide as you inhale and exhale through your mouth. Notice your eyes may water or you may want to yawn again and again. This is one of the natural ways your body attempts to relax itself. Notice how your body does this with very little effort. Your ability to relax has been built into your body since birth. It is always there for you.

Echo Breathing:

Sit up tall, relax your shoulders, close your eyes and imagine you are in a dark hollow cave. If you were to say hello out loud, you might hear your voice echo. Now, take a deep inhale through your nose and exhale out your nose. Listen to how the inhale and exhale echo each other. Exhale and then exhale again. Now inhale and exhale again. Play with the echo's of your breath and notice how they bring you into the moment.

Counting Breath:

Sit up tall, close your eyes, and breath through your nose with your mouth closed. If this is difficult for you, you can breathe with your mouth open. On inhale count silently to yourself (1,2,3,4,) and on exhale count silently to yourself (1,2,3,4...,5). Do this for three or four rounds. Relax and perhaps roll your shoulders around.

Physical Movement

Some students respond more easily to the breath through physical movement. Yoga or martial arts is an attractive doorway for motivating students to breathe. As a yoga teacher, I find it ideal as it accommodates students of all ranges and abilities. It requires no money and can be done anywhere at any time. It also works well as an adjunct to other physical types of exercises like hiking and walking. Consider teaching students how to breathe while playing on the play ground or walking in a field. You don't need to be an expert at breathing. By bringing your students attention to their breath you *are* strengthening their awareness.

#2 Tool: Incorporate Play

There is growing concern amongst psychologist about lack of play and face to face experience amongst today's children and adolescents. Through play students are able to learn to read social cues, develop empathy, take turns, and navigate their emotions. Play is also a natural remedy for anxiety, stress, and depression. The power of play was researched extensively by the famous developmental psychologist, Jean Piaget who stated: "Children learn more efficiently and are more knowledge when given the opportunity for play based activities such as: dramatic play, art, and social games" (Nager & Shapiro, 2005). I once attended a workshop on anxiety and depression with Dr. John Douillard, DC. Dr. Douillard is an author and director of the Life-Spa-Ayurvedic Retreat Center in Boulder, CO. Within the first ten minutes of the three day workshop he had the participants play kick ball. I was reluctant. I had not gone there to play kick ball, I did not want to play kickball, and quite frankly I did not want to waste my time playing kickball. Five years later, that kickball game continues to impact me. The point of the game was not to play kickball, but to recognize how play has the ability to lift you out of a state of depression and anxiety. The greatest lesson for me was at that time I had no idea how anxious I truly was.

If your students are prevented from play they too will become oblivious to what they are truly feeling. Anytime you can incorporate a bit of play into your teaching you not only increase self-awareness but also breaking down the walls of inner resistance. A lack of play builds inner resistance toward experiencing and trying new things.

Try This!

Incorporate Games. Games that require students to concentrate and tune into their own self awareness may be considered power tools.

» **I spy.** This game requires zero materials, just a focused attention on details in the present environment. Students are asked to search visually around the room for items that the teacher or student has quietly spotted. Don't be surprised if students naturally quiet themselves down as talking will decrease their ability to focus.

» **Jeopardy.** The teacher or another student provides the answers while the remaining students guess what the question may be. Jeopardy is a great way to review material for a test. Keep in mind the power comes from playfulness and connection to each other as opposed to from competitiveness. To maintain playfulness encourage students to work in teams. The entire team needs to be in agreement before an answer is stated. The role of stating the answer out loud is rotated amongst each team member.

» **What am I thinking?** This is a game I use in my self-esteem workshops with girls. This game sharpens self-awareness as each player is asked to retrieve information with their eyes closed. With vision and hearing eliminated, each player must tune into their senses, feeling, or inner knowing. Intuition has been referred to as a sixth sense. The development of this sense can help keep students safe. It teaches them to trust their gut instinct. In the classroom students are often encouraged to go with their initial gut answer. When students second guess or question their own abilities they may make unnecessary errors. Rachel Perry leads workshops on strengthening your intuition. She taught me the game below.

The game requires two players. Each player sits across from and facing one another. One person holds four pieces of different colored paper. The second player views the colors. Then each player closes their eyes. The player holding the colored paper says, I am sending it now to indicate he has chosen to focus on one particular color. The player across from him sits quietly with his eyes closed. When he feels ready, he attempts to guess the color. This game requires each player to quiet their minds, tuning into sensations they may be less familiar with. Another option would be for the teacher to show the class four colored cards and when ready state I am thinking of it now to the entire class. The class can have fun guessing the correct answer.

For six years, I co-taught parenting classes with my partner Cindy Horgan. If you work in a school you know how difficult it can be getting parents to attend such classes. However, for six years I watched our free parenting classes grow to the point where wait lists were necessary. Eventually, I ventured off into the mind-body field while Cindy continued to passionately provide these classes with solid attendance. What is the secret to her success? I believe she is perfectly aligned to her purpose in life and she has an incredible sense of humor. Through every day examples, she makes the material come to life. She is animated and playful in her explanations.

She manages to laugh at herself. What makes Cindy's humor a power tool is its stem from a place of knowing, accepting, and respecting differences.

#3 Tool: Review Progress

Reviewing progress teaches students how to direct their attention to the present moment. It is particularly helpful when students and teachers find themselves overwhelmed or pressured by expectations. Students learn through the process of reviewing progress how they can choose which thoughts to focus on. The experience of choosing what to focus on *is* part of the progress. While expectations of success and achievement still exist reviewing progress widens the scope allowing students and teachers to see how their awareness manufactures a sense of being. This plays a large role in future progress.

Reviewing progress is a free ride back to the present moment. Imagine yourself driving along the highway. You forget which exit you passed or what town you are in. You review the possible landmarks passed which requires more than your thoughts. You need to tap into your senses. Perhaps you recall a building or a piece of landscape. Perhaps you remember hearing a certain song on the radio while passing through a certain town, or maybe you remember the taste of your coffee around a certain exit. In that moment, you are in charge of the direction of your thoughts, guiding each one from a place of feeling.

Reviewing progress can be practiced at any time of day with any age group. I would suggest you make it a regular part of your class routine. When stress levels are high or students feel trapped or rushed by expectations, consider reviewing progress more than once in a day

Below are some examples written in the form of scripts. They represent a few ways to do this. As always feel free to change or modify according to your needs and teaching style. Don't be concerned if students remember things out of sequence or are unable to retrieve parts of their day. This is not a test but rather a way to experience moving back to the present moment.

Scripts for reviewing progress. When reviewing these scripts notice how thinking backwards requires a focused attention. Notice the difference between forward thinking and backward thinking. Forward thinking often has an anxious or rushed quality while backward thinking requires you to slow down and concentrate. One is not necessary better than the other. You are just programming yourself to feel rather than evaluate the difference.

Preschool. Okay, everyone. Can anyone remember the last three things we did? Let's remember together. Try to think backwards. You painted your picture, you picked a piece of paper, and you choose a paint brush.

With preschools it is helpful if the teacher holds up each visual, even walking backwards around the room to help students with this process. This exercise teaches focus and memory.

Elementary. Okay, everyone let's review our progress. Who can remember all the things we have done in the last hour? Well, you started by hanging up your coat, handing in your lunch request handing in your homework, gathering your materials for morning work, listening to the tasks for the day, getting out your math sheet, completing your math, handing it in, and going back to your desk.

This exercise reviews progress by recalling all the steps up to that point. Students are able to see the skills they have mastered as well as the value of process.

Middle / High School. Before we begin let's take a moment to acknowledge all the things that needed to take place in order for you to begin math today. First, you had to choose to get up this morning, eat breakfast, gather your materials, and find a way to school. You needed to have your homework complete and I am certain there are many other things and situations you had to deal with before this moment. Once you have acknowledged all of these things consider yourselves ready to begin.

Middle and high school students are starting to wonder who they are and what they have to contribute to the world. By reviewing progress you are allowing students to see a bigger picture of themselves. They see that each and every moment of their lives as significant in creating a bigger picture of who they are.

#4 Tool: Allow the Word "No."

The word No can at times feel like a rebellious remark from a teenager or a challenging struggle with a preschooler. However, when viewed as a power tool it is a sign of self-awareness. Individual likes, dislikes, agreements, and even disagreements all contribute to the process of getting to know yourself well. When the word no is viewed in this way students understand that It is ok to be themselves. Learning how to use the word No may also protect students from engaging in at risk behavior. A student who is able to say No, thank you, respectfully and confidently to his teacher may be more likely to say No, to later temptations such as drugs and alcohol. No sets a boundary and gives people permission to take care of their own needs.

In the movie *The Girl With The Dragon Tattoo*, there is a disturbing scene where the killer lures his victim quite easily into his home by offering him a drink. Once the killer ties his victim up he comments on how he ignored his own instincts, how "the power of offending is always stronger than the power of instinct." By encouraging and allowing the word No in your classroom you are letting your students know they have a choice. Power is the ability to recognize the choices available in all situations.

You may be rightfully concerned that allowing the word No indirectly reduces your expectations. However, when encouraged consciously and skillfully the word No empowers both you and your students without sacrificing effort. The key is watching *how* you ask questions. For example, imagine if you ask a student if he would like to make up his math test during lunch. The student says, "No." As the teacher you view this as lack of effort dismissing the answer as indifference. This affects your attitude and tone of voice as you replay, "If you don't make up the test you will get a zero." The student answers, "Fine." Consider that student is responding to your tone of voice. He takes the test but where did the motivation come from? From his own need to maintain his grade from the need to obey his teacher or possibly both. Be aware of how you ask questions and only ask questions that allow a yes or no answer when you are prepared to accept either choice. Had the teacher said, "Sam, you have two choices you can make up the test during lunch or before school tomorrow, either option will help you with your grade." When stated this way the student is empowered by the choice rather than influenced by the reaction. Both the teacher and student benefit when communication is consciously delivered.

How you view the word No influences how you perceive the dynamics in your classroom. Note the preschooler who tells his classmate "No" when asked to share or the middle schooler who says "No," when you suggest he work with another partner. By perceiving the word No in this way teachers encourage individuality, acceptance, and when taught skillfully, respect.

Try This!

Model how to say No

> » Teach students it is not so much what you say but how you say it. Model different situations where you say No using varying voice tones. Teach students how the impact of No is altered by eye-contact and body language. Give them opportunities to practice through role plays. Note: I see college level students who miss class or opportunities to improve their grade because they were too busy pleasing others.

Create opportunities for Yes or No answers. Some examples include:

> » Would you like some help or a suggestion?

> » Would you care to change your seat?

> » Are you satisfied with your paper or project?

> » Do you understand how to do this problem?

Allow the No. Try not to override the students no. If a preschooler does not want help with his coat avoid overriding his No by doing it for him. Do not give advice to a high school student who said No when you offered help.

Provide Two Choices. By providing two choices you remain in the driver's seat while empowering the student. For example, would you like to read at your desk or on the rug?

On the Playground. The playground can be challenging when specific students are not included in group play. Some schools go as far as stating that students are not allowed to exclude any child from play. In other words, they can't say no. Children being excluded from a group are at risk of feelings of rejection or loneliness. This may lead to a poor self worth setting the student up for at risk behaviors. It is important to teach tolerance by showing students the skills to allow different individuals into group. However, it is also important to help children identify when they can say no. For example, if you want to go on the swings and someone else wants to slide you can say, "No, thanks." Better yet, ask students to brainstorm what situations are opportunities to practice tolerance and which are opportunities to practice no. Point out the advantages of tolerance, as well as the advantages to being saying no.

#5 Tool: Rituals

Rituals differ from routines in that they prepare the student and teacher from the inside out. Rituals are often rooted in intention whereas routines are focused more on actions, tasks, or duties. Brushing your teeth, getting dressed, packing your lunch, or checking your e-mail may be some actions included in your routine. Rituals have a history of being connected to a deeper meaning. They tend to be more flexible meaning they can be planned or spontaneous. Incorporating rituals into your classroom encourages creativity, bonding, and a sense of community.

The Waldorf School community has a strong foundation for building character and values in students by incorporating a wealth of rituals into their educational programs. For eight weeks I had the pleasure of walking down the halls of a Waldorf school that services students from ages one to fourteen. As I passed each classroom I could see how each had its own unique ritual for beginning the day. I witnessed rituals such as passing a ball quietly, hand clapping games, singing, playing a musical instrument, serving raspberry tea, playing, giving thanks, and jump roping. At the time, I was participating in a mommy and me group with my two year old daughter. The mommy and me group contained one ritual after another including making muffins, setting the table, listening to stories, and singing songs. That was the first time I really *experienced* the difference between a routine and a ritual. I left the program feeling grounded, connected, bonded, and immensely grateful.

Rituals feel different from routine. They promote a sense of awareness and comfort from within. My ninth grade English teacher had the ritual of calling all of his students by the letter of their last name. At the time my last name began with a Z and I vividly remember he would always stand at the entry way of his door greeting each and every student with a Good Morning. His greeting for me was, Good Morning Z accompanied by a pat on the head. This same teacher showed up at the passing of my father in law's funeral. He was also my husband's English teacher. Nearly twenty seven years later his presence still provides the flavor of safety and reassurance.

Rituals have the potential to create lasting memories imprinting your brain and body with feelings of love. Classrooms are an ideal place to create and maintain rituals. They can add style, spirit, and uniqueness to the curriculum. I would suggest you begin by noticing the rituals that already exist. Do you greet your students a certain way? How do you begin and end your day? Are there any celebrations you participate in during the school year? If a student or teacher is sick or hurt do you offer any rituals of support? Below is a list of some ideas.

Try This!

» Study rituals. Rituals have a strong tribal and cultural history. Talk openly with your students about the cultural differences in weddings, funerals, or holidays. Notice how rituals play a strong role in healing and building a sense of community.

» One teacher created the ritual of students turning to their right to greet the person next to them with wishes for good day.

» Rather than bringing in individual Valentines, another teacher incorporated the ritual of each student receiving one large valentine. Each classmate had to write something positive about that student on their large valentine.

» My daughter's second grade teacher celebrated Chinese New Year by ordering Chinese food.

» In middle school two teachers who shared a door connecting their classrooms made a point of saying Good Morning to their own students as well as students the classroom next door.

» When students or teachers share a story or a personal item it may create a time to incorporate ritual.

» Many schools incorporate rituals such as school spirit day, songs, music performance, and community service projects.

» Begin or end your day with an inspirational quote, news, or story.

#6 TOOL: HIT YOUR REFRESH BUTTON.

When your computer gets stuck or stops working efficiently the refresh button may restore or renew the process. Everyone has many refresh buttons. They are among your power tools. This section explains where your refresh buttons are, how to use them, and the benefits of doing so.

There are many nerve endings in the lower lobes of your lungs. When activated these nerve endings provide you with a tremendous amount of sensation. When these sensations are experienced fully your mind and body are refreshed with energy, insight, and awareness. Refresh buttons are an ideal tool for sticky or tense situations. These situations are often charged with assumptions. Refresh buttons soften your judgments, allowing you to view a situation more clearly, and less personally. Judgment can prevent people from taking responsibility for their own feelings and perceptions. When taught to students, refresh buttons encourage them to experience, and own their feelings. When students are blaming or tattling on each other ask them to hit their refresh button. Often the blaming or tattling serves as a distraction from feeling. The next section shows you how.

To hit your refresh buttons nerve endings you need to focus on your inhalation. In order to tap into the nerves of the lower lobes of the lungs the inhalation needs to be strong and fluid. To inhale fully move your navel away from your body. Your belly will blow up like a balloon and you will feel the sides of your waist expand. Once you feel the sides of your waist expand keep inhaling until you feel your skin and perhaps even the hair on your arms or the hair on your head. Your breath is fluid you are not holding your breath. Therefore, when you feel like exhaling, go ahead and exhale. Take your time, try not to rush or judge your breath. Just do the best you can. The more you practice the more refreshingly natural your buttons will feel. When things feel natural, the windows of power open, allowing you to begin experiencing your teaching in ways unimaginable.

Refreshing a situation is like opening a window in a closed off room full of stale and stagnant air. When you find yourself thinking the same old thoughts, repeating the same old words, or dealing with the same old behaviors try refreshing your buttons. Once you learn, to appreciate this innate power tool you may teach it to your students. Below are two sticky situations where refreshing buttons are applied. This is followed by a (**Try This!**) practice using declarative language. Declarative language is a power tool in itself. You know something is a power tool when it works collaboratively with other techniques.

Frustration at Lunch

Spring was in the air and the seventh grade team was showing it through their loud, boisterous behavior. The team was asked to quiet down several times by the lunch monitor. They would settle down for a few minutes and start right back up again. The lunch monitor held the team back from going outside to speak to them about their behavior. The students sat while the monitor explained her concerns and frustration. The students then went outside where they would be retrieved by their classroom teacher. The lunch monitor notified the classroom teacher about the steps she had taken. As the classroom teacher led the students back to the room, they once again they became loud and boisterous. Knowing the students had already been spoken to the teacher stopped them and said they would be losing five minutes of their lunch the following day.

As you read the above situation perhaps your natural inclination is to judge whether this teacher handled this situation correctly. If you found yourself thinking that way, which I hope you were, try refreshing your buttons instead. Instead of judging this teachers reaction try relating to her situation. How might this teacher be feeling? What sensations may be surging through her body? Take a deep inhale and feel the situation. When you judge others you limit your potential to respond in a way that serves you and but others well. Had the teacher refreshed her buttons while listening to the lunch monitors situation she would have allowed herself to feel the tension rather than bury it. Burying feelings is like burying power.

Team Meeting Tension

> At nine thirty in the morning the following team members gathered to discuss whether a student was eligible for special education services: classroom teacher, speech pathologist, special education teacher, school psychologist, and mother of the student. The meeting was moving in a positive, productive direction until the mother started to fill in the team about the dysfunction of the student's father. The father was not present at the meeting so immediately the team members were cautious about how they responded. The room grew quiet as the tension increased. The meeting was no longer flowing but rather stuck in an emotional energy that felt quite disturbing. The team responded by listening and saying very little. The school psychologist handled the tension by giving a blanket statement of "That must be hard for you."

Working with families listening to their challenges and hardships is difficult. You may think that once the meeting is over those uncomfortable feelings will dissolve on their own. Feelings dissolve on the inside, not the outside. You cannot distract your way through. I remember going to a team member later on to discuss or process what had happened. In hindsight, that was my attempt to get rid of the tension that continued to reside in my body and occupy my mind. Had I refreshed my buttons I could have felt the tension fully during the meeting sending myself as well as other team members signals of safety and love.

TRY THIS!

Use Declarative language. Declarative language is ones inner speech the brain thinking about what it needs to do to complete a task. Sarah Ward is a speech and language pathologist who leads workshops on Executive Functioning. She states declarative language teaches students how to self-monitor, self initiate, and think independently. In the Frustrated Lunch example, rather than lecture students the lunch monitor could have chosen to use declarative language. In other words she could ask the students, if you were ready to go outside what would that look like? Or how would I know if you were ready to go outside? Other examples of declarative language that Sarah provided are:

You better get it done. vs. How is your pace?

Wash your hands. vs. Your hands look dirty.

Get your math book, and pencil out. vs. If your desk were ready for math what would it look like?

#7 TOOL: I AM LIVING MY DREAM.

Affirmations are statements verbalized or written in the present tense. They teach students how they can be in charge of their own thoughts. Treat them as a recording. If you were to record your own thoughts which thoughts might you chose. Thoughts are most powerful when they are rooted in love, presence, truth, and energy.

Some examples of affirmations are: I am confident in my abilities, My effort makes a difference, I am creative, I am effective, and resourceful. For students who don't yet believe they are confident, creative, or resourceful teachers may need to challenge their thoughts by asking questions such as: how do you know when you feel confident or what does creativity feel like? For example, when you play the beat of a song with your hands do you feel creative? Utilizing affirmations in your classroom increases the likelihood of positive emotions, self-motivation, risk taking, improved self-esteem, and the development of a strong I voice. Students receive hands on experience of what a supportive inner dialogue sounds and feels like.

Lady Ga Ga a musician and singer made herself famous by writing songs that inspire others without undermining her true feelings. Songs such as I am on the edge of glory or Born this way are expressions of who she is. Lady Ga Ga is important as she is an example of how affirmations are not about being perfect. Although they tend to have a positive tone they are more about affirming who you are in the moment than creating an illusion of where you want to be. Positive is good when it is authentic and truthful. If I notice that I am judging another person that is an honest self-observation. I then have some choices: I can keep judging, feel bad that I judged, ignore my judgment or state an affirmation to myself. The affirmation of, *the present moment feeds me*, may redirect my attention to where I am most effective. Judging is a reaction that moves you out of the present moment. Affirmations are a kind and gentle way to bring yourself back.

The classroom is an ideal place to incorporate the use of affirmations and self inquiry. Treat affirmations as you would a word wall or spelling list. List two to three affirmations on a bulletin board, chalk board, or poster board each week. Introduce them at the beginning of the week and have students repeat them out loud or silently to themselves at least once a day. If this is uncomfortable for you try putting a beginning and end to this exercise. Tell the class that for the next four weeks you will be rotating affirmations and stating them out loud daily. Let them know the intention behind the exercise. In the (**Try This!**) section I show you how to affirm your classroom rules.

Through mindful inquiry, drawing, journalism, or sharing students may explore self-reflection. Teachers can spark self reflection by posting questions such as: what do you think of when you look in the mirror or how do you thoughts support you in school? Author Loyd states, "you are who you are in your heart" (p.161). Teachers may be afraid or concerned that if they bring up feelings some students may act out or fall apart. In my experience students may be initially timid but once it becomes part of the classroom routine and culture they look forward to the experience.

> I post a question for each class that allows students to engage in introspection or self reflection. I may ask them to take a few minutes and journal about what confidence means to them. This provides me with a sense of their belief systems. I may ask them to close their eyes

and tune into their hearts. Once they draw their attention to their hearts, I ask them if their heart truly believes confidence lives inside of them. Many times students confuse confidence with perfection. In order to feel confident they have to master whatever they are doing or please others. Author Chris Howard states, "confidence is not something you get it is something you feel." For example, do your students feel confident knowing their names or that they can find their way to the lunch room? Through mindful questions you can show students how what they believe about themselves may or may not be true.

Try This!

Heart Vibration. The purpose of beginning or ending a class with a question that stimulates self-reflection is to raise the vibration in the heart. Higher vibrations provoke consciousness and emotions such as joy, patience, and love. These emotions help students see the good in themselves as well as in others.

Little hearts. For students too young to understand what it means to self-reflect, support their heart vibrations through art, soothing music, and imaginary play such as caring for animals and babies.

Affirm your classroom rules. Affirmations may be utilized as a way to reinforce classroom or school rules. Some typical rules include walk, one person speaks at a time, respect others, and keep hands and feet to yourself. Older students have rules such as: no cell phone, show up on time, be respectful. Below are some rules followed by examples of affirmations. Notice how affirmations offer two qualities of a power tool: awareness and presence.

RULE	AFFIRMATION
No talking.	I am quiet, I am listening.
Be on time.	I am mindful of the time.

No cell phone.   I clear myself from distractions.

One person at a time.   I am patient and tolerant of others.

Keep hands and feet to yourself.   I am kind, and respectful.

8 Tool: Teach Strategies for Self Doubt.

Doubt is a state of mind fueled by feelings of insecurity, fear, uncertainty, and confusion. Everyone goes through periods of doubt. Imagine you were asked to teach a grade level or curriculum you were completely unfamiliar with. Immediately, you may start to question or doubt your abilities. Similar to stress, doubt tends to nest itself in the chest area around the heart. It can feel heavy and constricting similar to a broken heart. When your students are experiencing doubt it may seem natural to want to boost them up, or make them feel better. Like all emotions doubt serves a purpose and when noticed without judgment has the potential to empower students. Lifting the veil of doubt opens the gateway for clear, innovative thinking. To express and implement innovative ideas takes courage. Implementing ideas after moving through doubt can be life changing. The next section shows how to identify doubt in your students and strategies for moving yourself and your students through doubt.

When you reflect on the word doubt what students come to mind? How can you tell they are experiencing doubt? What do they say? What does their body language look like? Is the student able to make eye-contact? How does doubt show up in their work? Does the student you are thinking of experience doubt in certain areas or subjects?

Doubt sounds like, I can't, This is probably wrong, This is not for me, I'm not good at.., or I'll never. It questions, *Am I good enough? Pretty enough, or Smart enough.* Doubt shows up in the body through rounded shoulders, head hanging forward, lowered gaze, distractibility, or shifting the eyes.

To help your students climb out of the depths of doubt try talking about it. An article written by Tamara Jones called *Michelle Obama Get's Personal*, reveals the first Lady's own history with self-doubt when told: "Princeton might be too hard for you." Michelle Obama states "It doesn't matter what your grades are if there's a message in your head that makes you think you can't quite do something, you can feed into that." She pushed through and learned she "could actually compete." There are many figures in history such as Prime Minister Margaret Thatcher who became great leaders due to their ability to move through doubt. Discussing role models and leaders shows students how a huge component of success is the ability to accept doubt as part of the process of moving forward.

Your job as a teacher is to notice doubt, provide opportunities for moving through doubt and trust your students' abilities to do. One way to do this is to tell stories, if you don't have a story to tell, try making one up. The story below is one I created.

Story Telling

Let me tell you a story about a boy named Jim. Jim loved to play baseball. He would spend hours in his front yard practicing pitching, and catching the ball. On the weekends he went to the batting cages and practiced hitting the ball as far as he could. Each time he would imagine himself getting a home run the crowd cheering. Then there were times when he would go to the batting cages and he would hit the ball poorly. When this happened Jim would get frustrated with himself, at times doubting his own abilities. He would say things to himself, *I stink at baseball.* Or *what is wrong with me?* During these times of doubt, Jim would try to remember the times when he was able to hit the ball so far he would have run two home runs in the time it took to retrieve it. To do this he pictured himself holding the bat in his hands. He imagined the weight of the bat, the coolness of the paint on his hands. He pictured his eyes focused on the ball his entire body positioning itself attentively. When he did this he found his mind became free from distracting thoughts. Before he knew it he found himself once again enjoying baseball rather than doubting his abilities.

The above story teaches students how *what* they focus on and *how* they focus can move them through doubt allowing them to experience confidence. More strategies for working with self-doubt are in the (**Try This!**) section below. As you read through the suggestions remember your role is not to get rid of or cheer your students out of their doubt. By doing so you are indirectly placing judgment. The suggestions are intended to provide the means for students to move *themselves* through doubt.

TRY THIS!

» Make time for movement or exercise. Exercise is a mood elevator. Encourage your students to stand up and move between tasks. Stretch or walk briefly around the room.

» Encourage students to drink water. Water not only keeps the brain working efficiently it serves as a mood stabilizer.

» Be mindful of unnecessary comparisons. For example one class to another, this may discourage individuality and encourage competition.

» Learn how to give and receive criticism (see next power tool).

» Notice when a student has moved through doubt, for example, Kelly, your ideas are flowing nicely you seemed to have moved through your uncertainty.

» Tell stories of courage and faith. One of the most compelling stories I heard was about a dog named Faith, who learned how to walk on two legs.

#9 Tool: May I offer you a Suggestion?

How and when you provide constructive criticism has the potential to instill lifelong skills in your students. When applied skillfully, constructive criticism through feedback provokes thinking, effort, and inspiration. Delivering feedback is similar to creating an art project. Sometimes you need to let parts of the project dry before applying the next layer. Students often need time to digest and try out suggestions before moving on. Constructive criticism requires deep thinking which is generated from an awareness of the present moment. By absorbing the moment first you increase the likelihood of responding to your students thoughtfully with ideas that are tangible, strength based, practical, and constructive.

Constructive criticism is used frequently in the classroom setting as a tool for guiding students toward a broader vision. Perhaps the vision is for your students to be proficient in recognizing their letters by the end of the year. Or, that each student will know how to write an essay well. It is typically delivered verbally and in writing alternating between individuals and classrooms.

How and when you deliver constructive criticism, impacts how it may be received by your students. If you deliver criticism when you are stressed or irritated, most likely it will influence your tone of voice and overall attitude. It may be better to hold off giving feedback until you feel more centered. You may even tell a student that you would prefer to offer feedback when you are able to focus completely on their work. Your ability to focus on the present moment is the best way for you to prepare students for the future. Guidance from the now directs students from where they *are* as opposed to where you would like them to be. It prevents you from creating expectations that may be impractical, unrealistic, or unclear.

To create guidance from the now refer to your guide foundation. Use language that focuses on the senses. Watch for vision, Listen for sound, and Play for touch. Below are examples for guidance from the now as well as guidance for the future. Notice the difference between the two. Notice how guidance for the future tends to imply judgment and right wrong thinking. Judgment inhibits both student and teacher growth as it tends to maintain the problem.

Examples of Guidance from the Now

» Watch how you are adding your numbers.

» Play with this paragraph.

» Listen to how the sentences sound.

» Fiddle with these colors.

» Check over your spelling. Check the directions.

» Listen for the theme.

» Consider.

» Notice the guidelines.

» Try.

Guidance from the Future

» You need to.

» You really should.

» You didn't.

» You forgot.

» You're not.

> *I once went to a pharmacy to develop my photos. The store clerk started to confide in me that a customer was upset and the store manager responded by asking the clerk: "What she could have done differently to please the customer?" She said, "The customer wasn't even upset at me, she was upset that these photo machines don't work well." She added, "These machines are old, there is nothing I can do about them." The clerk was infuriated by the store manager's response to her.*

In the above example, the store manager provided guidance from the future. The manager was most likely trying to prevent future complaints. Guidance from the future tends to view situations as potential problems. Guidance from the now views situations as an experience. Had the manager responded from the now, he might have said, "these machines are old until the situation changes consider watching how you respond to customer frustration. Try to be mindful of your words and facial expressions, if you need help come get me."

Constructive criticism is a power tool when it infuses both you and your students with the power of presence. By grounding yourself in the now, using language that taps into the moment, and seeing feedback as an experience, you increase the likelihood that you will provide tangible feedback that inspires effort, risk taking, and a focused performance.

TRY THIS!

Begin with the positive. Positive does not mean perfect. If you cannot find anything positive acknowledge the fact that they showed up for school that day.

Treat constructive criticism as an offering similar to offering a gift: may I give you a suggestion? Or Would you consider? Have you considered using the strategy?

Be genuine and encouraging. Thank you for showing me your work, this was hard for you, but you kept going opposed to praise that does not fit such as: you are awesome or you are the best.

Ask your students if your feedback makes sense and is helpful to them.

Allow differences of opinion, agree to disagree.

Keep suggestions brief, perhaps no more than three at a time. For young children offer one at a time.

Provide clear examples both visual and auditory of what you are looking for.

#10 TOOL: LA, LA, LA

For the last century scientists have been studying the effect of sound on the body. Parts of their discoveries include human body's composition of energy, atoms, and water. This make up causes any kind of sound produced or received by the body to send an internal vibration. This vibration rattles energy, water, and cells offering a harmless approach to responding to stress symptoms such as: inflammation, fatigue, distractibility, and low energy.

Teachers are sensitive to the sounds in the classroom as they can be both distracting and disruptive to student learning. Some students are able to filter out external sounds while others are not. When a classroom is silent surrounding sounds can sometimes amplify, making it more or less distracting, depending on the learner. Students with auditory processing or comprehension difficulties may struggle in environments where the teacher speaks quickly or the classroom tends to run more loosely.

When used as tools for stress management and learning enhancement certain sounds may serve as power tools. The sound of your voice, chimes, ringing of bells, music, rain outside the window, poetry, rhythms, or a story read with enthusiasm all have the potential to captivate students in the present moment. The present moment aids students in processing and absorbing information. When applied consciously, sound gives students the means to respond to their inward needs. Imagine a student goes to lunch and is reprimanded by the lunch monitor. The student returns to your class feeling irritated and angry about what happened. The student has a couple of choices. He can dwell on his thoughts and continue to be angry, he can ignore his feelings altogether and pretend he is fine or he can distract himself by talking to his friends. All of these choices support the reaction of choosing not to feel. Now, imagine the student returns to a classroom that is infused by the sounds of an acoustic guitar or harp. The sounds of the guitar trigger the student's feelings allowing them to flow. When feelings are stuck or ignored students are more likely to choose behaviors possibly providing a false sense of relief. Some of these behaviors include talking or gossiping with friends, distractibility, rushing tasks, teasing, or complaining. Sound is a simple way to acknowledge and respond indirectly to the inward needs of your students.

If you are a human being you have inward needs. All you have to do is take a drive in your car to see stress is a part of ordinary life. Teachers can support student growth simply by choosing not to ignore stress. Using sound is ideal because not only can it provide relief from stress, it also improves memory and comprehension.

Consider how letters are first introduced to students by singing the ABC's through nursery rhythms and the reinforcement of spelling words, vocabulary, and reading comprehension through voice flexion or exaggeration of sounds. Author Dr. Amen references Campbell's research on "toning (to make sounds with elongated vowels) balances brain waves, deepens the breath and reduces heart rate" (pp. 205). Notice if you sing the vowel sounds a, e, i. o, and u, holding each note you can feel the vibration in your body. Use of sound is so powerful it has proven to alleviate symptoms associated with trauma such as post traumatic stress disorder. Author Amy

Weintraub is at the forefront of teaching therapists how to introduce the use of sound into treatment programs with clients.

Using sound effectively requires curiosity and experimentation on your part. Begin by noticing which sounds already exist in your classroom. Which ones are soothing, which ones are stimulating. Listen to the tone of your own voice and the tones you may emphasize. This is not a time to judge or criticize your voice but rather to get to know your voice as a power tool. Consider alternative approaches to sound as a way to capture student attention, a wooden chime, rain stick, drum, or classroom chant. Anything with an extended sound helps students *feel* their way into the moment.

Try This!

"A..a....a....a...a." Ask your students to pay attention to where they may *feel* the sound in their bodies, as the "a" sound, when held, vibrates in the heart. By directing their attention back to their bodies you are directing them to the moment.

Play music at the end or beginning of your class during the transition time.

Song Suggestions

Don't Worry About a Thing by Tobias Froberg.
Bhava Gino Foti.
Anything by Eric Whitacre (a virtual worldwide choir).
Replenish, Aardvark Kids Relaxation Music.
Beyond Silence, The Relaxation Specialists.
Brand New Day, Joshua Radin.
All You Need Is Love, The Beatles.
Chant Music for the Soul, Gregorian Chants.
Dinner At The Sugarbush, (African drumming) by Brent Lewis.
I Can See Clearly Now, Jimmy Cliff.
Imagine, The Beatles.
Intention Earth, Rise Sound System.
Kind And Generous, Natalie Merchant.

#11 Tool: Mirror, Mirror on the Wall

You are part of a larger fabric of the many teachers that exist in your students lives. Each teacher has the potential to serve as a mentor. How your students choose to view themselves is often a reflection of the people around them. Through their example and ability to listen, mentors provide powerful reflections of inspiration, courage, support, and unconditional love. Foundations such as Big Brother, Big Sister Organization and Boy and Girl Scouts of America have compiled extensive research on the benefits of mentors. The findings consistently support that children from the most challenging circumstances have a better chance at transitioning into adulthood when exposed to mentors. This includes children from poverty, broken homes, and abusive backgrounds.

Mentors surface in classrooms through volunteers, helpers, peer leaders, and guest speakers. There are mentor programs such as book buddies, community service projects, internships, or retired educators. With clear guidelines and open communication mentors may alleviate the pressure of expectation on teachers. The simple act of a high school mentor reading to a younger student or a retired business man offering wisdom on how to create a business plan, may transform expectation into moments of appreciation.

Not all teachers are comfortable inviting guests into their classrooms. It requires some effort on your part, as most schools need to corey individuals who. Some teachers refrain from requesting mentor visits to avoid burdening others. However, mentoring is mutually beneficial, creating a cycle of giving and receiving. Giving back to the community connects people to purpose and hope.

Mentors are also available in books, or news articles. The children's book *Ferdinand the Bull* by Munro Leaf is a wonderful tale of a bull that didn't care about being like all the other bulls and found he was most happy smelling the flowers. Consider compiling a list of books that support values and characteristics a mentor would provide. Also, try tapping into mentors in your building. Consider a student who has learned to work through a reading disability such as Dyslexia or who has moved from another country. Students learning to play a musical instrument or who have taken on a passion such as raising money and awareness for a cause may be closer than you think. In my Powered by Me® workshops for girls I often invite mentors in from the community. I find the girls respond well to girls closer to their age.

> *I once attended a workshop on alternatives for Anxiety and Depression. A young woman raised her hand and shared her story about having such extreme anxiety as a child that the school eventually decided to shorten her day to accommodate her needs. The group was eager to hear her story. They asked questions about how she got through it and how she was doing now. Once the workshop ended, I approached the young woman and asked her to share her story with my girls groups. It turned out she was a nutritionist and found relief from anxiety by making significant changes in the kinds of foods she ate. Since my own daughters attended girls' workshop I was able to see how what I had been teaching them for years seemed to click more when spoken from a mentor. I believe my daughters were able to see themselves more clearly through the reflection of a mentor.*

The first lady Michelle Obama created a program for local high school girls exposing them to many women in the White House from different backgrounds. Obama states in an interview with Tamara Jones reported in a piece called *Michelle Obama Gets Personal*, that she told a national summit on mentoring that "Even though our children are connecting in ways we never imagined, you've got an entire generation of young people truly in desperate need of a friend. Someone they can trust an example they can follow."(More Magazine, p. 64).

Who are the mentors in your community? If you believe mentors are scarce they will be scarce. By viewing everyone as a teacher the availability of mentors becomes abundant. To keep the experience positive set clear guidelines. Let mentors know how much time they will have to speak. Ask mentors to let you know ahead of time three things they would like to share. Tell them the three things need to set a positive example for others. Ask your mentors to leave ten minutes for listening and responding to questions.

TRY THIS!

Who is your role model? Consider exposing females to women in the science and technology fields. Males may benefit from role models who share their emotions and follow their dreams despite if it's apparent violation of the man code. Both genders may benefit from mentors such as lawyers or judges who describe what it is like to defend and negotiate. Once the connection is made you may be surprised to find how readily available they are. Below are some things to consider when choosing a mentor.

1. Choose mentors who truly love their jobs or hobbies. Mentors not only communicate what they do but are examples of passion, strength, and belief in oneself. For example, I once had a photographer speak to my girls group. I choose her because of her story more than her skill. Her photography was a way to stay connected to her joy and get through difficult times in her life. She adopted a child with bi-polar disorder and photography became a tool for being with the stress of raising a child with this diagnosis. She only took pictures of things and situations that brought her joy.

    I also had a mother of five speak to my girls groups about a trip to India where she worked in an orphanage. She brought pictures of her trip and showed them what they had in common with girls across the world.

2. Only choose individuals who are eager and willing. If you have to convince them or it feels like work this will reflect on the overall experience.

3. Notice the people around you mentors are everywhere. When I found out my babysitter was doing an internship with Meryl Lynch I immediately considered her for a discussion on investment talk.

4. Keep the visit short and allow time for questions and comments. I have learned not to fill the time up with lecture. Students

want to ask questions and directly interact with guests. I think thirty to forty-five minutes is plenty.

Tool # 12 Strengthening Social Skills

The influence of technology in the social world has created a new area for skill development. Students who have received little guidance or supervision in the tech world are now at risk for obtaining employment, and college entrance. Applicants have been turned down due to inappropriate facebook posts, rending social skill development more than etiquette. It is a way of being mindful of yourself and others.

The more aware students are of themselves, the more likely they are to interact with others in socially conscious ways. Examples of social skills requiring self-awareness include waiting in line, listening, engaging in a conversation, being honest, offering, and accepting criticism, taking turns, interrupting, offering, and accepting an apology, responsibility for oneself, regulating emotions, setting limits and boundaries, playing and serving others. The classroom is an ideal setting to strengthen these skills. Below are three things to consider when supporting the development of social skills.

1. Pick one to two social skills to focus on at a time. As a teacher it may at times feel exasperating to try to notice or address all the skills you hope to teach. Focusing on one social skill at a time allows creating a deeper experience with each skill rendering, you more likely to see and reinforce many variations of the skill. For example when waiting for a turn some students may stand close by, while others may go off and do something else. Each of these variations are neither right or wrong. Both represent the skill of waiting your turn.

    When I teach at the college I tend to begin the semester by focusing on the skill of trying something new. I do this by vocalizing and honoring the courage it takes to try a new class or new teacher. The next time I meet with the students I may expand on this by asking them to briefly reflect on another time in their lives when they were able to try something new. When you first learned to ride a bike, drive a car, or swim. My intention is to remind students through their feelings of what it is like to move through discomfort and perceived obstacles. By the end of the semester I am focusing on the skill of serving others and building community. This evolves quite naturally as I watch students support and talk openly with each other.

2. Ask questions. There are two questions that spark the inquiry of self awareness: How do you know? And what feels right? Both questions direct students to reach within themselves for the answers. Rather than tell my students when to breathe I often pose it as a question asking, how they know when it is time to breath? The students are less likely to rely on my verbal direction and instead they are nudged to look to their own internal and external cues. Internal cues include elevated heart rate and over thinking. An external cue is distractibility and forgetfulness. In the classroom a teacher may ask how students know when it is time to wait for their turn. Or, how they know when it is an appropriate time to interrupt. If a student asks you what to do in a certain situation you may respond by asking them, what feels right? Often students attempt to make decisions based on what is expected of them or whether they are meeting the approval of others. Asking them what feels right encourages them to develop their own inner guidance.

3. Use Visuals. Visualization helps students connect to the feeling behind social skills. The use of visualization allows students to imagine themselves utilizing social skills. When technology is overused as a primary form of communication students may lose opportunities to learn how to develop essential skills for maintaining healthy relationships such as trust, honesty, and communication. For example, a teacher may ask students to visualize through mental images and pictures, what it looks like to be a good friend. The teacher may ask, what can you picture yourself doing with a good friend, how would you

communicate, would you spend time together, how would you handle a disagreement?

The above three suggestions are ways to develop social skills in the classroom setting. For students who rely primarily on technology as a form of social development the three areas below are ways to counter balance the affects. When used in the classroom setting they are a means of connecting students to their wholeness, offering presence, and dismantling the hold outside influences press upon students today.

Counter Balancing Overuse

As a teacher you may notice how prolonged or compulsive use of technology creates an atmosphere of disconnection, at times contributing to physical symptoms such as eye strain, poor posture, and distractibility. Below are three practices. The first Bounce Back, is a way to wake up the breath to help clear the mind and open the heart. The second, Imagination leads students back to the present moment and the third Open Discussion offers students opportunities to discuss common pressures, ways to create balance, and foster inner strength.

Bounce Back

Bounce Back may be used anytime you notice students are unmotivated, distracted, impulsive, stressed, or burnt out. Ask your students to rub their hands together rapidly for fifteen seconds. This will create friction between their hands. Have the students place both hands side by side a few inches from their heart and take two deep breaths. See what the students notice. Perhaps their hands feel tingly, their jaws begin to loosen, and their breath starts to flow. You may suggest they move their hands around in a circle, toward and away from their heart to see if they can still connect to the vibration. Other variations put the hand in front of the forehead, throat or belly. Notice how this exercise invites students to breathe deeply without any direction from you.

Imagination

One of the best ways to increase motivation and loosen the grips of attachment to technology is to incorporate assignments and opportunities that tap into a student's imagination. Albert Einstein said "Imagination is more important than knowledge. For knowledge is limited to all we know and understand, while imagination embraces the entire world, and all there ever will be to know and understand."(www.thinkexist.com). Ways to utilize imagination in the classroom setting include: role plays, themes, art, projects, writing, make-believe, and visualizations. Teachers who feel pressed for time can activate imagination before or after transition times. You may ask younger children to imagine they are walking in a parade on a windy day. Before taking a test you may ask older children to put their heads down on their desks for one minute. Ask them to visualize moving through the test with ease, their breath flowing freely, their shoulders relaxed, their pencils moving swiftly, facial muscles relaxed, their minds free from distraction. After a test you may encourage students to detach from the test by imagining something completely unrelated. Perhaps have them picture themselves taking a walk in the woods, drawing in the sand, or cooking something that smells wonderful such as bacon or muffins. Notice how using your imagination activates the breath, stimulates the sensory system, and connects students to the present moment.

> *I have witnessed some preschools allowing use of the computer first thing in the morning when children's minds and bodies are fresh. Many times the student using the computer generates an audience of observers. Students hover, glued to the screen, waiting for their turn. The research continues to be strong that children learn social development best through imagination and play. Consider eliminating the use of technology first thing in early childhood programs.*

Open Discussions

Open discussions are a great way to alleviate the pressure students face in the classroom and technology world. Teachers may find themselves holding back from creating dialogue concerned that it may take them off track or bring up issues they are not prepared to deal with. However, open discussions are a great way to loosen the grips of attachment or mental distraction. Below are three things to consider when generating dialogue.

1. Opening up dialogue does not always mean you have to say the right thing or have all the answers. You may respond by saying, thank you for sharing or that is interesting.

2. Focus on what *is* working rather than what doesn't work. For example, you may ask if anyone wants to share helpful tips for getting homework done, staying focused on an assignment, or share a visualization that helps them get through stressful times.

3. Have students remember a time they felt focused or were able to exercise self-control. For example, how they keep themselves from eating an entire bag of Halloween candy or how they turn the television or video game off when they have homework to do. What might they say to themselves in those moments?

Try This!

Participate in Screen Free Week (April 30th- May 6th). This is a wonderful week where communities come together to provide experiences that are screen free. If you go to www.commercialfreechildhood.org. You can sign up for a free week organizer kit. The idea is to help families develop habits that give more time to reading, playing, movement, and exploration outside.

Play red light, green light. Red light, green light is a game that teaches awareness of breath. When the light is red students are to pause their movement for three seconds while continuing to breath. When it is green students continue about their task moving while breathing naturally. Try using this strategy as a way to teach students how to pause before pressing the send or search button on the computer, raising their hands, or giving answers. Notice how this delay makes students aware of the moments they may be unconsciously holding their breath.

CHAPTER 8

The Empowered Teacher

THE EMPOWERED TEACHER VIEWS HIS own consciousness as a resource for balance, security, and strength. Every experience viewed with consciousness is an investment in the educators self-awareness which powers the implementation of classroom tools, curriculum, and responses. It allows each educator to display his uniqueness, as the attention to his inner needs sets the stage for empowering others.

This chapter offers eleven components for stepping into the empowerment journey. You do not have to do anything. There is nothing for you to purchase, prepare, or prove. There is no final exam, time line, grade, evaluation system, prerequisite, or graduation. Your awareness is enough.

> "We must act on the assumption that we already possess that which we desire, for all that we desire is already present within us. It only waits to be claimed." Philosopher, Neville Goddard, June 17th, 2011.

Component #1: You have Arrived

The first component of your empowerment journey is adaptation of the belief that you are already an empowered teacher. This may feel foreign to you as a teacher who is trained to work with specific requirements before moving forward. You may feel as if you need a model, lesson plan, or instruction booklet. How do you measure whether you are ready? In education, a lack of readiness may be misconstrued as weakness or failure. Assume you are ready and consider you have arrived. You cannot fail. In fact, moving in and out of the empowered teacher perspective only makes you stronger. Each time you disconnect from the belief that you are there you are given another opportunity to strengthen this belief.

Your arrival has no destination. Therefore it cannot be measured or identified in the typical ways such as when you arrive at school. Your arrival as an empowered teacher happens every time you breathe, with each inhalation, and exhalation. It is strengthened each time you set an intention. As long as you are living and breathing you are an empowered teacher. If you do not feel the empowerment of your arrival it is because you have chosen to direct your awareness to other things. By paying attention to your breath you utilize it as transportation to your inner world. Your inner world is rich with sensations, images, thoughts, feelings, energy, and intuition. If you become distracted by your thoughts during this process perhaps feeling stressed or rushed, it is okay. Your thoughts and feelings matter. However, what matters more is your willingness to go along with the sensations produced in the present moment.

> *Amy was a part time Spanish teacher due to her hours having been cut over the past couple of years. Her part time hours left her feeling disconnected and less valuable than other teachers. These thoughts seemed to fester in the back of her mind, making her feel less certain about her current position as well as her effectiveness.*

Amy viewed her part time hours as an indication that she was less than and separate from other teachers. Her thoughts strengthened her feelings of isolation creating distance in her experience of bodily sensation. Your arrival into the empowered teacher role is not based on what is happening outside of you but rather what is happening inside. Had Amy focused on her breath when thoughts or feelings of insecurity rose she would have shifted herself from creating a story to creating an experience. A story is anything you tell yourself over and over such as: *I am only a part time teacher* or *I only work at one school*. These stories hold you back from recognizing and receiving your arrival. You may prevent yourself from receiving the moment because you feel you have not yet done enough.

You know you are viewing yourself as having already arrived when you begin to feel full. It is like having a big meal and feeling completely satisfied. You find yourself paying more attention to what you *do* have, as opposed to what you don't. You are able to notice former measures of empowerment such as test scores or approval from others, during your experience rather than allowing them to determine your experience. Outside measures no longer control your inner world. Each time you utilize the tools that ignite your awareness, such as breath, you are reinforcing the belief in your arrival.

TRY THIS!

Your are rich. Teachers serving in poor communities may benefit from redefining their image of wealth. If you see yourself or your students as poor, you generate vibrations that relate to being poor. You and your students are rich. Your wealth is your sensations. These riches are massively available to you at any moment. The fact that some of your students may be poor is not necessarily the problem. The problem is whether they view themselves as poor. See yourself as rich, bathe in your riches, and allow yourself to become an image for wealth.

Re-activate Your To Do List. Instead of writing down your to do list try noticing your sensations first. Allow your inner experience to dictate what you put on your list. Notice if it changes how you write things down. Notice the level of importance, intensity, and order. Is there anything you may have left out or disregarded had you not experienced your sensations first?

COMPONENT # 2: TEACH FOR YOU

Teaching for you is a way to bring the focus back on yourself. When you teach for others for the main purpose of meeting expectations or demands such as curriculum, district, and state requirements you are more likely to draw your attention away from you. Teaching for others is tricky because when you do meet the expectations of others you may feel a sense of relief and pride. Relief feels good, so it would make sense that you would strive to meet more expectations to feel it again. Seeking relief is like going on a diet. You lose a couple of pounds feel great and then gain a couple of pounds and feel crummy.

Teaching for you directs you back to your present moment. Expectations do not live in the present moment. In the present moment, your awareness opposed to the act of seeking relief feeds you energy, vitality, and focus. You expand into your goals rather than gain relief from your goals. With expansion there is no need to pick yourself back up and dust yourself off to start over again. In essence you become growth from all experiences, not just the positive ones.

> *While writing this book I attended a workshop lead by author Edward J. Langan on the relationship between self-esteem and the law of attraction. During the break, I spoke to Langan about my experience as a first time writer. I told him it is such a private experience and the idea of releasing it to the world felt overwhelming. His advice to me was, "Write the book for you, no one else but you." I started to notice the times I would think about how others would respond to my work. When this occurred my writing felt less fluent and more like a thing I needed to complete. When this occurred, I would state to myself, write it for you. This immediately tuned me into my breath shifting my focus to my sensations. My sensations became like a faucet releasing the flow of my writing.*

Once I started to write for me, as you will teach for you, I was able to identify parts of my day when I disconnected from the intention. Consider reflecting on the moments you are teaching solely for the purpose of others. Imagine you are at a curriculum meeting listening to expectations and requirements. Watch and listen to how you respond to this information. Do you start to think about all the things you *have* to do? Notice if you start to feel pressure and where that surfaces in your body. Notice if you have trouble sitting still or paying attention. The information you receive about yourself in that moment tells you if you are teaching for you or if you are teaching for others. In that moment shift the awareness back to yourself. Say to yourself, Listen for you. Allow this statement to shift your attention back to your breath. Allow your breath to trail into your inner sensations. Feel the sensations that you formally distracted yourself from. Notice the feeling of pressure. Now, notice if anything has changed. Do you feel lifted or drained from the information that is being presented? Look at these types of meetings as opportunities to practice teaching for you.

Try This!

Learn for you. I once asked my daughter why she went to school. Her response was "To learn and because I have to." I said to her, "What if I told you to learn for you, no one else but you?" She replied, "But mom, you would have to be really strong to do that, I mean, I have been told forever to learn it for the school."

Try this experiment on your students. Consider telling your students to learn for themselves, no one else. See how they respond. This will provide you with insight into how much of their motivation comes from within.

Component #3: Body Whispers

The empowered teacher utilizes the language of his own body as a resource for guidance, resiliency, and strength. The language comes in the form of body whispers. Body whispers are communicated through your outer physical body as well as your inner subtle body. Some whispers may be quite loud communicating through physical symptoms such as headaches, stomach aches, tension, back pain, or leg pain. Inner body whispers speak more softly through the language of sensation for example, through tingles. Outer body whispers influence inner body whispers and inner body whispers influence outer body whispers. When outer body symptoms, such as headaches, are ignored, it may lead to imbalances in the inner body such as high blood pressure. Separating your inner and outer body is similar to handling a problem between two students by only talking to one. You only hear half the story and therefore your perception of the situation may not be clear.

Learning how to listen and interact with your body whispers offers you clarity, energy, and self-confidence. You are less likely to experience your bodily symptoms from the perception of a victim. The more you practice hearing these whispers the more you realize how much you play a role in the outcome.

> *Judy was a veteran teacher who loved teaching until about four years prior. When I asked her what had happened over the past four years she spoke of a new curriculum director who put a tremendous amount of stress upon teachers. As a result Judy felt an enormous amount of stress which gave her physical symptoms such as: fatigue, bodily tension, and trouble sleeping. I spoke to Judy and asked her how she planned on taking care of these symptoms and she replied, "Retire early."*

In the above example, Judy became a victim of her circumstances causing loss of stamina and desire to teach. Had Judy choose to listen to her body whispers, she could have relieved her stress, and fed her body with vitalizing energy. The circumstances may not have changed however her thoughts and perceptions most likely would have. When you see things differently, you alter your experience with what you see. Author Bruce H. Lipton provides scientific evidence in his book *The Biology of Belief* that perceptions whether they are true or false, are beliefs which in turn control biology (p. 135, 2005). Your thoughts communicate with your cells and your cells communicate with each other. There is no separation. The good news is your cells are constantly regenerating themselves giving you opportunities to reinvent your experiences.

How to Listen to your Body Whispers

Most people are fairly good at hearing their outer body whispers. However, if you are busy you may not hear your inner body whispers as well, if at all. Below are some steps that will help re-train you in how to listen to your body.

1. Notice the difference between hearing and listening. Imagine hearing a bird. You hear the bird and perhaps wonder *what bird*

that is or *where the sound came from*. Now, imagine listening to the bird. Notice how to truly listen. There is very little thinking involved. You have to concentrate and be in the moment.

2. Now apply this to your body. Hear your body first. Perhaps you feel tight or restless. You may think thoughts such as *I have no time* or *I am going to be late*. Now listen to your body. Notice the tightness in your shoulders and keep focusing your attention on your shoulders while breathing. Notice any thoughts or mental impressions that come up. Notice how within a few minutes the sensations from the outer body blend with the sensations of the inner body, becoming one. In the beginning you may find this exercise easier to do when you are alone. With practice you will be able to listen to your body whispers even when your students are around you.

3. Listening means freeing. Freeing your body whispers allows you to interact with your body as opposed to react to your body. Your mind, body, and spirit become one and with that come the power to make decisions from energy and clarity rather than from a state of brokenness.

Some of your greatest teachers come in the form of curriculum directors, principals, students, or staff. In a way, everyone is a teacher and everyone is a student. Listening to your body whispers is like being the student. Your body is the teacher.

Try This!

Wake up to your whispers. Notice how you wake up in the morning. Do you begin your day with thinking or feeling? Try setting the tone for your day by listening to your body whispers while lying in bed for an extra moment or two. Scan your body from head to toe with your eyes closed. Listen with full attention for at least one minute. Do this for several days and see how it impacts your day.

Component # 4: Tend to Your Spirit

Tending to your spirit is an act of surrender. Each time you take a breath and observe yourself consciously you are tending to your spirit. This allows your teaching to unfold naturally in the absence of limitations. Consider your perception of time. You may feel constantly short of time to meet expectations required by your position or curriculum requires. As a result you may feel rushed or inattentive. Tending to your spirit gives you a new concept of time as well as other obstacles such as expectation, money, and support. These concerns do not go away they are simply replaced by a greater interest and desire to experience the current moment fully. Full experience of the moment nurtures your spirit, which is not subject to boundaries or limitations. Your spirit is looking for you to relax and flow with your moment rather than resist it. Your spirit offers you a gentle reminder that every situation and experience has something to offer. As a result extenuating circumstances currently beyond your control receive less attention from you. Tending to your spirit not only reserves energy it increases your ability to respond to situations without losing power.

> *Mary Ellen was a second grade teacher. She had twenty-three students in her class many of whom had significant learning and behavior challenges. As a result, a teacher's assistant was placed in her classroom daily until noon- time. When the assistant was present Mary Ellen felt supported and effective. However, when the assistant left, Mary Ellen viewed her departure as a great loss. She would now need to spend more time managing and less time on teaching.*

In the above example, Mary Ellen is most likely draining her teaching ability by holding on to her previous experience with the assistant. Holding on to what you had, or could have had, or don't have enough of may drain you. This in no way is meant to dismiss or play down Mary Ellen's situation. She may in fact need more support. However, getting the support you need does not need to come at the price of your zest, strength, and creativity. Had Mary Ellen chosen to tend to her spirit it may have lead her to valuable insight and lessons the present situation had to offer.

How to Tend to your Spirit

Breathe consciously noticing your inhale and noticing your exhale. Do this when you find yourself with a few minutes of alone time. Allow your breath to flow naturally while you watch your response. Notice how you feel inside and notice the world around you. If you are in your car, notice the trees, sky, or anything connected to nature. Do this for as long as you like. It is more helpful to tend to your spirit consistently daily for a few minutes opposed to once a week for fifteen minutes. After a few minutes, return to your daily life consciously. If you were in your car begin to walk into your school while continuing to notice the world around you. Who do you see along the way? What do you see in the environment? Can you pick up on any patterns or things that appear to be coincidental? Maybe a specific person or parent is on your mind and you suddenly run into that person. These types of coincidences and patterns may be a way your higher consciousness is communicating with you. Perhaps connecting with this parent will help you with your current situation.

TRY THIS!

Play with this statement: I am open to what this situation has to offer me. When you find yourself overwhelmed by a situation try stating the above statement out loud or silently. You may even want to write it down or journal about it. Tending to your spirit is about opening yourself up to the possibility that your higher consciousness has something to offer you.

COMPONENT # 5: NOTICE YOUR MODELS OF EMPOWERMENT

Models of empowerment are examples of living in the present moment. Anything that is living and breathing can be a model for empowerment. Some examples are animals, nature, your students, your children, and co-workers. Each time you witness one of these models you reinforce *how* to be in the now. The process of witnessing triggers your own self-awareness. Your self-awareness guides you back to your power.

> *It was a typical Monday morning. The car was running as I quickly ran back and forth from the house with items necessary for the day. I checked off each item in my head: Back packs, check, Coats, check, Water bottles, check, Cell phone, check. My nine year old daughter was sitting on a rock looking at the sky. She said, "Look Mom," as she pointed to the top of the tree. "That is the one who is doing all the singing." She added, "Look how he shakes his tail when he sings." I looked up and saw a little bird at the top of the tree. It wasn't so much what she noticed that made an impression on me it was how she noticed it. Her body language and the way she gazed at the sky. She appeared focused, peaceful, and at ease. At that moment, I received two models of empowerment. The first was my daughter and the second was the tiny bird. I turned to my daughter in the car and said, "Thank you for that Mikayla, that is exactly what I needed today."*

Models of empowerment are particularly beneficial on the days you find tuning into your moment extremely difficult or you are too busy to notice whether you are in the moment or not. By making yourself aware of the models that exist around you, you are expanding your support system. This less direct support system helps you to retrieve your moment. Perhaps you notice two students playing, a student drawing, a tree blowing in the wind, the flower on your desk, rain drops falling on the window, the laughter or whistle of a co-worker, or a squirrel collecting nuts. Anything that is alive shares the same vulnerability of being easily influenced by its environment. You and your models of empowerment are more connected than you may think.

TRY THIS!

Take a walk. Consider taking a walk outside your school building.

While walking, look, and listen for models of empowerment. Even if you are not sure whether what you see is a true reflection of what it looks like to be in the moment, continue to notice. Empowerment models may be as distinct as someone reading a book to a more obscure model such, as an ant in crawling the dirt. The more you notice the more you realize you are surrounded by images of presence.

COMPONENT #6: CONNECTING ENERGY

Connecting energy is a way to tone down the intensity or stress of a situation by focusing on feelings that promote connection. If you work with another teacher with another teacher whose style is more carefree than your structured approach, you may feel uneasy, uncomfortable, and somewhat stressed. Some typical reactions may include thinking about the differences, focusing on what bothers you about the other teacher's style or distracting yourself with busy work. When this happens, try focusing on the feeling opposite of what you are experiences. For example, if you sense control or power, focus on the energy of acceptance. The blending of these two energies that allows them to co-exist.

> *Twice a week Mrs. Williams went into Mrs. Field's class for forty-five minutes to teach students how to answer questions properly on the state mandated tests. Mrs. Williams had a very different teaching style from Mrs. Field. She was more strict and sharp with the students. The students would often complain when Mrs. Williams left the room. Mrs. Field dealt with her discomfort around Mrs. Williams by crossing her arms and keeping her mouth shut. When Mrs. Williams would show Mrs. Field her way of teaching, she would disagree inside but on the outside she stood silently. Mrs. Field often felt exhausted by the experience, since she was the one who had to deal with the students complaining after she left.*

In the above example Mrs. Field choose to react to her feelings by keeping silent. Had she chosen to connect energy instead it would have looked something like this:

> *Mrs. Williams enters the classroom and begins instructing the students. Mrs. Field watches how she responds to Mrs. William's presence. She notices immediately that she is thinking far more than feeling. She makes a conscious decision to connect energies. She does this by paying attention to her own sensations. She takes a deep*

inhalation and begins scanning her body, stomach, arms, legs, and neck. In some areas she feels tingly while in others she feels dull. This takes only about a minute. While noticing her sensations she notices how her focus shifts less on Mrs. Williams and more on herself. This subtle shift of perception moves her into a less reactive state. She is now open to the idea of connecting energy. Her own sense of peace allows her to see the peace inside Mrs. Williams. Now they are connected.

Connecting energies is a technique allowing the experience of your sensation to shift your perception to one where you can experience an emotion that promotes harmony. This technique may be practiced anytime, anywhere, and with anyone.

To Connect Energies:

1. Feel your feelings. Notice the sensations in your body, tight areas, or frequency of your thoughts. If your thoughts are firing off quickly most likely you are feeling very little. Take some full breaths to connect with your body over your thoughts.

2. Notice how your attention shifts away from what is happening outside of you to what is going on inside.

3. Tune into your connection generating emotions such as, relaxation, love, compassion, and peace. Make a personal dedication to the person who helped you recognize your own disconnection to self such as may you have peace, love, or compassion.

4. Honor Opposition. Opposition many times is the force individuals need in order to make a shift in their perception. If you were always in synchronicity with those around you, there would little opportunity for growth.

Try This!

Sensation Smoothie. Treat yourself to the experience of sensations. Imagine your feelings are food and your sensations are nutrients. Close your eyes and visualize yourself in your kitchen with a blender. Watch yourself fill the blender with all the feelings you experienced that day. A little frustration, dash of joy, and a pinch of worry. Continue to close your eyes and imagine the sensations and gifts those feelings have to offer. For example, frustration offers the gift of motivation. Once you have everything in put the lid on top and see yourself press the on button. Feel the vibration as you watch the mixture swirl around. As you inhale, drink your smoothie and receive the nourishment from the ingredients that came from your own inner garden.

Component #7: Teach to Serve

Teaching to serve is a way to motivate your teaching. It keeps you connected to a sense of purpose offering you balance. It does not matter whether you are servicing one student or a full classroom. Your conscious choice to serve sends a message to you and those around you that you have something to offer. By treating your teaching position solely as a job or work you may be confining yourself to predefined roles, duties, and tasks. This may limit your potential and subconsciously drive you toward a need for perfection. What you have to offer is much more than what you do. It is who you are. You are energy and when you intend to serve, the energy generated from your emotions expands you from inside out.

Imagine you are running late, you have a team meeting first thing and have yet to give the substitute teacher the assignments for the first hour. You pass several students and adults in the hallway, give a quick hello, but charge forward until you get to your classroom slightly out of breath. Seeing your students' faces (your empowerment models) and hearing their greetings begin to ground you but you quickly take yourself out of the moment because in your mind that will only lead to more delays. You have tasks to take care of and responsibilities to get to.

The above example illustrates what it is like when teaching is another form of doing. Doing pulls you out of your moment while service connects you to being. You may think if I do this task I will feel better and I will be free from stress. The empowerment perspective differs as the present moment is seen as a source of freedom. You gain the energy and focus you need to go about your day from the present moment. When you approach your teaching with this perspective you realize that you have something to offer every minute of the day. Your contribution is not contingent upon achieving specific tasks or accomplishments. Just by sitting still or smiling consciously at a student you are contributing your peaceful energy to your surroundings. Service comes from the energy of the heart, while doing your job comes from your brain. Your heart holds a powerful energy capable of uplifting your performance without depleting your internal resources.

Doing	Serving
Keeps you out of the present moment.	Connects you to purpose.
Depletes energy.	Connects you to others.
Disconnects you from others.	Gives you energy and focus.
Creates more thinking.	Ignites passion, resiliency, and strength.

TRY THIS!

Choose your focus. Rushing and thinking repeatedly about what is next are signs that you are pulling away from your power. While it is impossible to stop your thoughts it is possible to choose which thoughts to focus upon. Shift your attention to what is happening around you. Notice your students smiles, the sounds in the room, and watch how noticing promotes focus. It *is* possible to move swiftly through your day without losing power. When you feel rushed trust your inner guidance to lead you to the resources and knowledge suitable for that moment.

New perspective on no shows. If a student's parents or caregivers are not showing up to school events or meetings refrain from thinking they don't care. Not showing up may signal the person feels they have to little to offer. Tell them how showing up offers a message of commitment, respect, and partnership.

COMPONENT #8: GETTING TO GRATITUDE

Moving into the empowerment perception has much to do with moving into gratitude. The practice of gratitude has been well documented by science as a viable means for creating happiness, resiliency, and inner strength. It is a way to build yourself from the inside out as it has proven to boost your immune system and increase the flow of feel good hormones all of which lead to a better quality of life. Nathan DeWall, who has led several studies on gratitude, stated "It helps people become less aggressive by enhancing their empathy."(John Tierney, New York Times, November 21, 2011). This practice is ideal for supporting all students, particularly those struggling with low self-esteem in the classroom setting. The question remains how does one get to gratitude? If you are exhausted, overworked, feel unsupported, or just plain crappy how do you get to a place of giving thanks?

Gratitude is much more than the act of saying, thank you. It is a way of appreciating the present moment as it *is* as opposed to how you may prefer or hope it to be. Getting to gratitude is however, a process. It includes learning a bit about your subconscious mind and speaking less from your brain and more from your heart. You may find it hard to appreciate a student who drains every ounce of patience out of you. Teachers who feel consumed by a few students often experience guilt and resentment for having less time or less energy for the remaining students. Anytime you feel less than you are speaking to yourself as if you are divided into pieces. The process of getting to gratitude is less about *doing* and more about *being* who you are. Being who you are is highly connected seeing the *whole*. You are energy which envelopes mind, body, and spirit. Being connected to your wholeness allows you to see in every moment there something to be grateful for. It may be as subtle as the colors in your room, the smell of coffee, or the food on your plate. It is always there.

Your Inner Flow

When the reflections of gratitude which are always in front of you, seem invisible you may have to jump start your inner flow. Your inner flow is how your body brings itself back into balance through blood flow, circulation, and emotional energy. Your blood flows through every organ in your body, nourishing your cells, muscles, and bones. As you breath blood is related to your life force. When your breath and blood flow is constricted your mind may also become constricted. Nourishing your blood and breath is one of the ways to offer yourself balance and widen your perception making gratitude a more tangible option.

To nourish your inner flow:

>> Choose foods that are clean and offer elasticity to your blood flow. Whole foods, organic (no chemicals) with bright colors are some of the best choices green leafy vegetables. Learn to *love* eating well. In the beginning eating well can feel like a job or a chore. Play with your food, allow yourself to become interested in varieties, recipes, restaurants, and markets.

>> Get centered. Practice centering yourself through breathing before a meeting, in between tasks, grading work, and answering a phone call. Take three deep breaths and imagine your feet are becoming rooted into the ground like the roots of a tree. Picture yourself receiving an earthly energy. One of the best places to practice this is outside on grass or soil. The more you practice the more likely centering becomes your life rather than a part of your life.

>> Drink plenty of filtered water. Author and science journalist Lynne McTaggart states "A dry mouth is one of the mind's first early warning signals of danger." (p. 139).

» Feel your emotions. For individuals who are chronically tense or feel tight try getting a massage, receiving energy work such as reiki, taking a warm bath, counseling, acupuncture, or yoga. This may help you tune into your emotions allowing them to flow through you with awareness.

» Cardio exercise. Walk, run, bike, hike, do anything that gets your blood, heart, and breath pumping. Notice how the practice of gratitude comes more easily after you exercise.

TRY THIS!

Notice from the Whole. Think about *all* the people who were involved in meeting your student's needs in just one day. Pick one need that was met. Did your student eat today? Think about what needed to happen to provide your student with the food on his plate. Someone needed to grow the food, pick the food, a driver needed to transport it to a store, a business supplied it to your school, where someone mostly likely cooked and prepared it. Consider all the individuals involved providing your students with pencils, paper, computers, and art supplies. Noticing from the whole helps you to see the big picture, you are not alone and there is much to appreciate.

See your inhale as a creative breath. Many of the tasks required of educators including report writing and documentation may seem mundane. Think of these tasks as mini projects. Projects imply a process needs to take place. In this case, the process is your breath. The beginning of the inhale stimulates creativity, the middle of the inhale opens to truth, and the end of the inhale is your potential. Your exhale brings you back to the task at hand. As you approach the task imagine your body continues to exhale on its own. Watch how your breath transforms rote tasks into creative moments.

COMPONENT #9: SURRENDER YOUR JOB

Surrender your job is a way to imagine, accept, and move through any uncertainty you have about your job. This uncertainty may be holding you back from reaching your true power. Uncertainty robs you of vital energy, security, and creativity. Learning to move through your uncertainty not only elevates your potential but opens up the doorway for attracting the kinds of people and situations that you desire to be around. In other words, if you desire to have a principal that values and supports you, you must generate energy that attracts those types of qualities.

Allowing yourself to experience your fears and uncertainty is a way to increase your energy. By ignoring, repressing, or distracting yourself from those experiences, you are depleting your energy bank. Your energy gives off a frequency of vibration. This frequency finds a match. For example, the frequency of fear may attract situations that are critical in nature. To do this, simply allow yourself to experience uncertainty. Notice the sensations you experience when you think uncertain thoughts. Perhaps there is very little sensation, it does not matter, just notice while breathing deeply and you will move it through. Moving it through, as Zoe Marae states, generates energy. Working with your emotions in this way may not always change situations. However; it will alter how you experience them.

> *I was once called into a school to teach stress reduction techniques to a small group of teachers. The group talked about how stressful their jobs were and how they often felt unappreciated. One of the main teachers was strongly considering resigning from her position. I worked with the group for three weeks, twice a week for one hour helping to guide them through their experience. After three weeks, I went in and they were all smiling at me. I said, "You are all smiling what is going on?" Two of the staff members they had been complaining about decided to leave their positions. The two individuals that replaced their positions contained the qualities they desired.*

It does not matter whether you are a teacher or CEO of a corporation. No one has complete certainty when it comes to job security. Notice any signs of temporary or false relief from these kinds of fears. Perhaps someone gives you a compliment or comments on your efforts and suddenly you feel on top of the world. Often these boosts are short lived. Long sustained relief comes from reenergizing yourself through your own self-observations and experiences.

TRY THIS!

Notice when you feel uncertain or fearful where you feel it most in your body. Notice any tightness in your chest, mouth, or shifting of your eyes. Draw your attention completely to one of these areas and hone in on it using your breath. Try not to push against or force the feeling out. Just notice the sensation and allow it to move at its own rate.

Feel the fear. Allowing your feelings to move through means accepting them for what they are. Imagine what it would feel like to lose your job. Just imagine. You might feel confused, shocked, upset, sad, or overwhelmed. Often it is not so much fear of the situation, as fear of feeling the pain of the situation. Feeling your feelings does not make them come true. Try communicating to the feeling of fear instead of to the thought of fear. Do this through your breath. Communicate with your inhalation and communicate with your exhalation. Notice the difference between feeling your feelings of fear and thinking fearful thoughts.

Altering your perception of fear and feeling your feelings of fear frees you from fear. Author Harriet Lerner said, "Only after we know that we can live without a relationship-and feel entitled to make that choice-can we think, speak, and act clearly within it."(*The Dance of Connection*, (p. 121). Realize your job is not about what you lose but rather what you gain when you allow yourself to feel fear. Consider yourself gaining the ability to speak up, be creative, and teach with ease.

COMPONENT #10: CREATE INTENTIONAL GATHERINGS

The idea of creating intentional gatherings amongst teachers in schools came to me after I became familiar with author Lynne McTaggart's research on the power of intention. Intentional gatherings are a sacred place educators may assemble to set intentions into motion. For example, if exams are pending educators may want to set the intention that the students and staff be free from distractions, anxiety, and stress. According to McTaggart, studies indicate, "Your current state of mind carries an intention that has an effect on the life around you."(p.155, 2007). The finding that caught my biggest attention was the feedback researchers received from both the sender *and* the receiver of the intention; both reported positive effects from the experience.

If I were to design an ideal teaching environment intentional gatherings would be at the top of my list. A gathering can occur with two or more individuals who are interested in sending out positive thoughts to the world around them. These gatherings are ideal for individuals who feel challenged by the idea of sitting still and directing their focus. The sender of the intention receives the benefit of practicing positive thoughts in the now and the receiver is supplied with comfort, compassion, and love. I see this type of gathering benefiting individuals who are truly struggling. Perhaps students that may be experiencing pain, loss, health impairments, aggression, or insecurity. I realize confidentiality may be an issue. Although being specific with your intentions does appear to make a difference, you may send out thoughts of compassion to a particular classroom in a building. Visualize the class using kind words, working calmly excited about learning, taking turns, and improving their grades. Before students take a test visualize students working with ease, taking risks, and working confidently. Intentional gatherings may also find a place in the beginning of the school year. Inviting staff to take part in a collective consciousness where the ideal working environment is visualized.

Guidelines for creating an intention gathering:

1. Find a space that is quiet and comfortable. Sit participants in circle.

2. State the rules of the meeting arrive and end on time, keep names of individuals' confidential, work in silence, set intention into motions through breathing, and concentration. Consider setting a timer for ten minutes or more.

3. Take a few minutes to relax, adjust the temperature of the room, and play soft soothing music.

4. Ask if anyone has a specific intention they would like to focus on. For example, I would like to send the intention of acceptance and patience to a third grade boy in this building. Or I would like to send thoughts of gratitude to the parents of the children in the building.

5. Work with one intention per gathering. Keep intentions concise and in the present moment. Imagine it as if it were already happening. Feel in your body and see through your own eyes what it would be like if the parents felt appreciated. What would patience and acceptance feel like? What images or colors come to mind?

6. Develop an ending ritual. A hand on your heart, bow your heads, hold hands, take a breath, ring a bell, anything that feels comfortable to the group you are working with.

Component #11: What's Love Got To Do With It

Love is the energy of many emotions such as: compassion, empathy, joy, kindness, peace, excitement, creativity, and passion. Even your darker emotions such as depression, anger contain seeds of love. It does not matter what you feel. It does matter how much you allow yourself to experience what you feel. Your guide foundation (chapter 2) gives you the means for this experience. Consider a time when you were physically present in your classroom but your energy was dispersed between the past and future. In that moment you were being directed by your thoughts. The *energy* of love can only be experienced in the present moment. You may have a memory of love but the experience of that love is in the now. Teaching from the now is a way to teach from love.

The Benefits of Teaching from Love

The more you teach from love, the better you feel. The better you feel, the less relevant things that previously weighed you down become, while teaching from love does not keep you from experiencing emotions such as loss, guilt, or pain, your perception of those feelings may change. Your emotions become who you *are* rather than an obstacle to who you would like to be.

> *Sarah was a third grade teacher who was asked by her principal if she would consider looping to the next grade with some of her students. Although she loved her students and the idea of looping the thought of moving on with some of her more challenging students concerned her. For three weeks she ruminated over what to do. Who would she take with her and how would that impact the remaining students? Finally, her principal asked her to look at the situation in a different way. Rather than thinking of individual students her principal suggested she try looking at the class as a whole. This advice was very helpful to Sarah. She was caught up in the details and by looking at her class as a whole Sarah was able to receive her own wholeness. Experiencing her wholeness (all of her emotions) brought clarity allowing her to focus on decisions that benefited both her and her students.*

In the above example, Sarah was originally paralyzed by her thoughts. By looking at her class as a whole, she was able to move through her thinking into feeling. Her feelings offered her clarity and guidance. Love does not come and go, your presence comes and goes. To teach from love does not mean you have to be happy or positive all of the time. It is a willingness to feel things deeply so you can receive your inner guidance.

In the empowered journey there is no difference between giving love and receiving love. It is not based on that. It is a love that allows both giving and receiving to intertwine and flow *within* each other rather than side by side. Therefore, it cannot be measured by a mental checklist. In the book, *Dying to Be Me*, author Anita Moorjani speaks of her near death and healing journey with cancer. One of the many blessings she received from her journey was the gift of clarity. She writes about receiving the understanding that "to be me is to be love."(p.139). Below is a practice that intertwines the *energy* of giving and receiving. Consider applying this practice before or after mundane tasks such as grading papers, or writing a report. You may be surprised to see how well you are able to maintain the energy of love despite the task in front of you.

TRY THIS!

The Love Twist. The energy of love is a unique blend of giving and receiving. This practice teaches you not only how to experience these two energies but how to maintain them through a focused awareness on what you choose to receive.

1. Begin with three breath cycles. Each breath cycle contains a full inhalation and a full exhalation.

2. Once you can feel your bodily sensations you *are* in the present moment (try not to second guess this). Honor your moment by being open to receiving it. Do this by allowing *all* of your sensations to surface; even the uncomfortable ones such as nervousness or agitation. This too may be done in three breath cycles or more.

3. Begin to dissolve any uncomfortable sensations through your body with your exhale. Do this by taking an inhale and an even longer exhale. Imagine all of your unpleasant sensations dissipating. Imagine exhaling through your eyes, nose, ears, and face.

4. See yourself receiving fresh oxygen, blood and energy. Your fresh energy offers you a blend of inner calm, with mental alertness. Allow this heart energy to lead you into your task.

Maintaining yourself as an empowered teacher requires you to learn how to live with stress. Techniques for living with stress are included in the appendix of this book.

FULL CIRCLE

Your self awareness benefits everyone. Your student, caregivers of your students, other staff members, and most importantly, it benefits you. It supports your ability to teach, learn, heal, and love. In Chapter One I described power as self-awareness. If power is self-awareness and love is a form of self-awareness, then to be in your power means to *be* love. Now that you have reviewed the ten components of the empowered teacher hopefully you recognize that the empowered teacher has lived in you all along. It does not matter how long you have been teaching, where you teach, what you teach, or even how well you teach. You are power. Your self-awareness offers you stability, stamina, and inner peace.

On New Years Eve, 2011, I spoke to a high school teacher who taught in the inner city. I asked him questions about his job and listened to his experiences as a teacher. He looked at me and said, "I wish I could rekindle the romance of it all." He was referring to his love for teaching. I asked him what he believed was getting in the way. He spoke of the school culture how some teachers were working hard while others appeared to do very little. Over the last sixteen months I have contemplated our conversation many times. I can honestly say at the end of this experience I believe it is possible to maintain your love for teaching, and love for learning simply through the cultivation of your self-awareness. In fact, I believe you can do anything, get through anything, and still maintain a sense of inner peace simply by tuning into your awareness.

You were conceived and born with self-awareness. It is infused in the make-up of your mind and body. The only difference that exists between one person's self-awareness and another's is how much one chooses to value it. To value your awareness means to love yourself fully. The romance, my friend, lives in the journey of loving yourself well.

Until next time, be well, be aware, be love.

APPENDIX

ADDITIONAL TECHNIQUES FOR BOTH STAFF AND STUDENTS

The following exercises connect students and staff to their bodies. This builds the foundation for mindfulness practices. Connected breath, body guide, muscular release, press pause, stretching, guided visualizations, storytelling, along with specific breath techniques for students with attention difficulties are amongst the list. Choose the ones that feel right for you and practice.

As always please consult your doctor before attempting these techniques. Do not attempt these techniques if you are pregnant or have any serious health conditions.

Connected Breath. Practice developing your breathing by connecting to something that is living and breathing such as, a plant, tree, or bird. Imagine yourself breathing with the bird, or breathing with the tree. You may not be able to visually see a tree breathing but perhaps you can feel it.

Breath practices for ADHD: Students with ADHD may benefit from a breathing technique called, *Breath of Joy*. Breath of joy, like medication for ADHD is a stimulant. Karen, a third grade teacher used it with one of her students and found positive results. This breath technique requires movement of the arms so be sure your students are standing and have room to move. It requires three inhalations and one exhalation. On inhale their arms extend over their heads, then inhale again (no exhale) with the arms out to the side, then inhale a third time with the arms over head. Finally, exhale the arms down by their sides. Each movement is done swiftly and the inhalations are through the nose while the exhalation is through the mouth. Do three to five rounds and end the practice with your students standing still for twenty seconds as they feel their own vibration.

Breath and Heart. The chest openers below support individuals who feel hurt, insecure, or powerless. Before applying any empowerment strategies it is important to connect students and staff to their hearts.

Chest Openers

»   Sit upright in a chair toward the back of the chair. Place your feet hip width apart on the floor. Interlace your hands behind your back. Press your knuckles down toward your tail bone while sitting up tall. Spread your collar bones away from each other to widen your chest. Take a few long deep breaths.

»   Sit all the way to the front of your chair. Straighten your arms and grab the back seat of your chair. This action expands your chest while stretching your arms and shoulders. Take three to five deep breaths into your belly.

»   Sit up tall toward the front edge of your chair. On exhale, give yourself a big bear hug, grabbing the backs of your shoulders. Open your arms wide and receive the wealth of the inhale. Change arms and once again give yourself a bear hug, open your arms wide. Notice how your jaw naturally loosens and your back teeth separate.

Body Guide. Now you see how raised consciousness and increased body focus go hand in hand. Notice your body's built in capacity for inner guidance. Watch your students take on a writing assignment. Often you see students stop perhaps lean back in their chairs and pause. Notice if you interpret this pause as an indication of being stuck, disinterested, or frustrated. Writing is something that comes from inside. Pausing, leaning back in the chair, or putting down a pencil may very well be the body's way of positioning itself to receive information from within. By watching your students without judgment you promote heart responses.

Muscular release. Attends to stress by gathering the tension in the muscles and then releasing it. Through deep squeezing (contracting) and releasing actions the body is flooded with a rush of relief. To do these contract the areas of the body that are condensed with nerves such as the face, fingers, cheeks, and lips. Squeeze these areas tightly for ten seconds, as you release feel how the volume of your in breath increases. This is a great way to reboot the breath and relax tense muscles.

Press Pause. Imagine you have a button located slightly above your navel. This is the place where our ego tends to live. The ego is impulsive, quick to protect itself, especially when individual pride is at stake. As you exhale tug on this button by drawing your navel toward your spine. Pause for one count and then fill your lungs on inhale. This should take about three seconds. Pay close attention to the sensations in your mid-section. As these sensations disperse watch how fearful thoughts (ego) transform into sensations of comfort and love.

Stretching. Attends to stress by lengthening your connective tissue and fibers. When you are tense you are less sensitive to the sensations brought to you by your inner and outer world. One of my college students once asked me, "What do I do if I believe my fearful thoughts?" A big part of changing your belief system is tuning with your body. Through stretching and conscious breathing you are creating space between thoughts. Once this occurs the number of thoughts automatically decreases. This makes modifying the quality of thoughts more obtainable, meaning you get to actively choose which thoughts to focus on. Below are some stretches you may incorporate into your day.

Spine Stretch

» Place your hands on a wall shoulder width apart and walk backwards until your spine is at an angle. Spread your fingers wide on the wall pressing evenly through each finger. Keep your head even with your spine and feel the stretch in the back of your legs. Hold for three to five breaths.

» Sit in your chair with your feet parallel on the floor. Keep your hips even and very gently twist toward the right and then toward the left. Try not to initiate the twist from your neck or shoulders. Twist on exhale and release back to center on inhale. The twist will not be deep. If you are feeling like your twist is minimal you are most likely doing it well.

Forward Fold

Stand with your feet parallel and a little bit more than hip width apart. Soften your knees. Interlace your hands behind your back and press your knuckles down toward the floor. Spread your collar bones. You should feel this in your upper back as opposed to your lower. On inhale open your chest and on exhale begin to slowly move forward with your eyes open the entire time. Pause when you are half way down. If you do <u>not</u> feel dizzy feel free to drop your head below your heart bringing your arms up over your spine. Take three breaths and then on exhale bring yourself back up to standing. Release your hands.

Samples: Guided Visualizations and Story Telling

The guided visualizations below are a tool for maintaining your position in the guide role. You may read the visualization out loud in a small group setting or to yourself. Consider picking a time of day that is less active such as the beginning or end of the day. Included are guided visualizations you may read out loud to your students. In the beginning, your students may feel uncomfortable with this exercise. However, through consistency and repetition they will begin to seek the experience of their own bodily sensations.

Your Are an Empowered Teacher

Sit comfortably, close your eyes and take a deep inhalation and a deep exhalation. Relax your face and jaw. Imagine the color yellow. See images of various hues of yellow through nature such as flowers, a sunrise, or sunset. Visualize the bright color yellow circling your body. See it swirl around your feet and watch it travel up between your legs, torso, and arms. Imagine it is penetrating your skin with sensation. Breathe deeply and support this process by continuing to notice your lips and jaw. Release your back teeth, allowing your lips to slightly part. As you slowly inhale and exhale you begin to feel the power of your own body. Your skin cells serve as millions of antennae picking up signals of internal strength, compassion, and comfort. Keep breathing and notice. It is not necessary to try or put great effort into this movement. You already have everything you need. This is your time to watch how you are being guided in this direction. As you envelope this feeling, realize the true power behind your classroom goals and efforts. Your goal may be effectiveness and your intention may be connection. The partnership between your goals and intentions fuel the process. Take a few more moments sealing this moment inside of you. Complete the union between your goals and intentions by placing your hand on your heart and making a silent dedication to a student, family, fellow teacher, yourself, or to the planet.

Guided Visualization before Administering a Test to Students

Sit up tall with your feet flat on the floor. Close your eyes and roll your shoulders up toward your ears and down. Notice when you do this, how your inhalation becomes stronger. Now bring your right ear toward your right shoulder and then your left ear toward your left shoulder. Notice any tension you may have in your jaw or mouth. Just notice. Now sit up tall and with your eyes closed, shoulders relaxed, bring into your mind a time you felt confident. Notice any pictures that come to mind. Perhaps you feel confident when you ride your bike, climb, listen to music, play, read, or draw. Tune into your feelings of confidence. What does it feel like in your body and what might you say to yourself. Allow yourself to experience those feelings of confidence as if they were happening right now. Notice the fullness and flow of your breath and the softness in your belly. Keep breathing and on your next exhale open your eyes, once again notice your feet on the floor. Notice the paper in front of you, the pencil in your hand. When you are ready, you may begin.

Note: I would strongly suggest you introduce this guided visualization a few times before the actual test. Spend no more than three minutes on it. Students are typically anxious to get the test over with. It is the consistency of these types of practices that lead to progress. Guided visualizations increase blood flow, improving memory, and learning.

Story Telling
Challenging Moments

Sit up tall, with your feet flat on the floor and close your eyes. Imagine you are walking in your neighborhood. It is a beautiful sunny day. Out of the corner of your eye you see an orange cat. The cat's spine is arched, his mouth is wide showing all of his teeth and his fur is standing up. In front of the orange cat is a black cat, growling, also with a flexed spine, fur extended. You think, there is going to be a cat fight. You wonder what to do. Do you yell and scare the cats away or do you stay clear of the situation? Before you can respond you see one of the cats walk backwards, put his tail down and run in a different direction. Cats obviously cannot talk things out so how do you suppose each cat figured out what to do? They listened to their bodies. They listened to the fear, felt the fear and let their bodies guide them through a difficult situation.

Think of some difficult situations you may come across in school. Perhaps when you are taking a test, have a disagreement with a friend, or are sitting in a class you find absolutely boring. Think about how you help yourself through those situations. Do you think about how much you hate taking a test, or how your friend is no longer your friend? Does this help you to feel better?

Remember the cats and let your body guide you through. Notice if your shoulders are forward or up. Relax your shoulders, your jaw, and neck by moving it side to side. The cats sensed fear. Just by listening to the story, you may have sensed fear. However, the fear is not real. There are no cats and therefore there is nothing to be concerned about. You have to tell your body there is nothing to fear. The best way to do that is to bring yourself into the present moment. Notice your breath, if your skin is tingly, lips are tight, or if your breath is shallow or full. Just notice. Watch how noticing your body *is* a way to communicate to your body: relax, breath, and let go of fear thoughts or worries.

References

Ahlers, Amy. Interview with Lisa Garr, *The Aware Show* June 8, 2012. www.theawareshow.com.

Amen, G. Daniel. M.D. *Change Your Brain Change Your Life: The Breakthrough Program for Conquering Anxiety, Depression, Obsessiveness, Anger and Impulsiveness.* Three Rivers Press, New York, New York, 1998. The effects of positive thinking on the body. 40, 58, 75, 205.

Brookfield, Stephen D. *The Skillful Teacher: On Technique, Trust, and Responsiveness in the Classroom.* Second Edition. John Wiley & Sons, San Francisco, CA. 2006. 28.

Bridges, William. *Transitions: Making Sense of Life's Changes.* Preface to the 2nd Edition, pg xii. Da Capo Press, 2004.

Baker, B (1992, March). *Children and Transition Time.* (ERIC Document Reproduction Service WO. ED 35145). Retrieved July 11, 2008 from ERIC database. Retrieved by Timothy J. Fox, Concordia University of Portland.

Big Brothers and Big Sisters Organization. www.bbbs.org.

Bridges William, Ph.D. *Transitions: Making Sense Of Lifes Changes*. 2nd Edition, Updated and Expanded. Da Capo Press, 2004. xii and 4.

Campbell, Don. *The Mozart Effect*. The Mozart Effect Resource Center. www.mozarteffect.com/InThe News.

Carey, Benedict. *Evidence that Little Touches Do Mean So Much*. New York Times, New York Edition. Print version Feb 2012, D5. Online version Feb 22, 2010.

Challem, Jack. *The Food-Mood Solution*. John Wiley & Sons, Inc., Hoboken, New Jersey, 2007. 4,5.

Cherry, Kendra. *The Five Levels of Maslow's Hierarchy of Needs*. Abraham Maslow, "A Theory of Human Motivation" 1943. www.about.comguide.

Chopra, Deepak. *Reinventing The Body, Resurrecting The Soul: How to Create a new You*. Harmony Books, New York. 2009. Inside cover of book.

Chopra, Depak. "Prepare for the future by being in the now." Master Class. Own Network Television. April 2012.

Conklin Martha T. PhD, RD; Laurel G. Lambert, PhD, RD, LD, and Janet B. Anderson, MS, RD. A summary of three studies: *How long does it take students to eat lunch?* The Journal of Child Nutrition and Management. A publication of the school nutrition association. Issue 1, Spring 2002. www.schoolnutrition.org.

Dwyer, Wayne. "You get what you are not what you want." Interview Dr. Wayne Dwyer did with Oprah Winfrey on Super Soul Sunday. OWN Network, May 27, 2012.

Delaney, Brigid. *The Benefits of Laughter*. Article posted on CNN (articles.cnn.com), June 4, 2007. American College of Cardiology cited in the article.

Engel, Beverly. *Honor Your Anger: How Transforming Your Anger Style Can Change Your Life.* 93, John Wiley & Sons, Inc. 2004.

Eliot, Lise. Ph.D. *Pink Brain Blue Brain: How Small Differences Grow into Troublesome Gaps-and What we Can Do About it.* Mariner Books, Boston, New York. 2010. 6,7, 158.

Fehmi, Les, Ph.D, and Jim Robbins. *The Open-Focus Brain: Harnessing the power of attention to heal mind and body.* Trumpeter Books. An imprint of Shambhala. 2007, 19.

Ferlazzo, Larry. *Helping Students Motivate Themselves: Practical Answers to Classroom Challenges.* Eye on Education, 2011.The information used for this book was from Larry Ferlazzo's blog: www.larryferlazzo. edublogs.org.

Forbes, Bo, PSY D. *Yoga for the Nervous System,* 2008 held at Kripalu Center, Lenox, MA. She is also the author of, *Yoga for Emotional Balance: Simple practices to help relieve anxiety and depression.* Shambhala Boston & London. 2011.

Fox, Timothy J. *Effective Transition Techniques.* An Action Research Proposal Report Presented to the Graduate Program in Partial Fulfillment of the Requirements for the Degree of Masters in Education / Continuing Teaching License. Concordia University, Portland, 2009.

Goddard, Neville. *Change the world.* Neville Radio Lecture. June 17, 2011. Radio Talk Station KECA, Los Angelos. www.nevillelecturehall. com.

Goleman, Daniel. *Working with Emotional Intelligence.* Bantam Books, New York, New York. 1998.79, 164.

Gurian, Michael. *The Wonder of Girls: Understanding the Hidden Nature of Our Daughters.* Atria Books, New York, 2002. 33,34.

Hartenstein, Matthew. *The Power of Touch.* A conversation with reporter Diane Sawyer, World News, abcnews.go.com. Feb 23, 2010.

Hatfield, E., J.T., & Cacioppo, and R.L. Rapson. *Emotional Contagion. Current Directions in Psychological Science,* 2, 96-99. 1993. www. elainehatfield.com

Hillier, Mazza Gina. *Everything Matters, Nothing Matters: For Women Who Dare to Live with Exquisite Calm, Euphoric Creativity and Divine Clarity.* St. Lynn's Press, 2008. Excerpt from www.life. gaiam.com.

Holloway, Daw J. *Advances in Anger Management: Researchers and practitioners are examining what works best for managing problem anger.* American Psychological Association. March 2003, Vol 34, No. 3. Print version: 54. www.apa.org.

Horgan, Cindy. M.S. Edu. Parent educator. Cindy contributed several stories and insight to this book. Cape Cod Children's Place. chorgan@capecodchildrensplace.org.

Howard, Christopher. *Turning Passions into Profits.* John Wiley & Sons, Inc. New Jersey, 2004. 144.

Jones, Tamara. *Michelle Obama Gets Personal.* More Magazine: For Women of Style & Substance, pp. 64, 66. Feb 2012. www.more.com.

Kain, Eric. *High Teacher Turnover Rates are a Big Problem for America's Public Schools._*Published on line March 2011.www.forbes.com/ sites/erikkain/2011/03/08/high-teacher-turnover-rates-are-a-bigprob.

Kariuki, P., and R. Davis. *The Effects of Positive Discipline Techniques as they Relate to Transition Times in the Middle School Classroom.* November 2000. Retrieved, June 25, 2008 from ERIC database.

Keogh, Barbara K. *Temperament in the Classroom.* Baltimore: Paul H. Brookes, 2003. Information found in Harvard Educational Review. www.hepg.org/her/booknote/65.

Kristal, Jan. *The Temperament Perspective: Working with Children's Behavioral Styles.* Paul H. Brookes Publishing Co., 2005. 83.

Langan, Edward J. *Change your life: Self-esteem and your belief system* workshop. February 2012. Osterville, MA.

Lama, Dalai. "If you want others to be happy, practice compassion.""If you want to be happy, practice compassion." www.brainyquotes.com.

Leaf, Munro. *The Story of Ferdinand*. Viking, A division of Penguin Books USA. Inc.

1936.

Lerner, Harriet, PH.D. *The Dance of Connection: How to Talk to Someone When You're Mad, Hurt, Scared, Frustrated, Insulted, Betrayed, or Desperate*. Harper Collins, 2001.

Lin, Kelly. *Goals versus Intention*. Posted on www.squidoo.com. Kelly Lin is a certified life coach, www.lifecoachrocks.com.

Lipton, Bruce H. PH.D. *Biology of Belief*. Mountain of Love/ Elite Books. Santa Rose, CA. 2005. 135. www.BruceLipton.com.

Loyd, Alex PH.D and Ben Johnson, MD, DO, NMD. *The Healing Code*. Grand Central & Life Style, Hachette Book Group. New York, NY. 2010. 161, 177.

Marae, Zoe PH.D. A biological scientist who did research at Harvard Medical School in Boston, MA. Dr. Zoe Marae leads virtual workshops. "Emotions are not the problem, it is the non-movement of emotions that lead to disease." This quote was taken from a lecture held on Cape Cod at Changes Salon, Summer 2011. Dr. Zoe Marae also coined the technique of "calling judgment broccoli." Chapter 1, www.thriveyoga.com.

Maregni, Karen. Karen is a third grade teacher at *Avery Elementary School* in Dedham, MA. She is referenced in the appendix section as well as other examples where breathing techniques were utilized to calm children down.

Martinuzzi, Bruna. *A Firewall for Bad Mood; How to Prevent Emotional Contagion.* www.openforum.com. Powering Small Business Success. Co-author of *The Leader as a Mensch: Become the Kind of Person Others Want to Follow.* Martinuzzi and Michael A. Freeman, M.D. 2009.

McCraty, R., D. Tomasino and R. Trevor, *The Heart Has It's Own Brain and Consciousness.* Mindful Muscle. www.mindfulmuscleblog.com.

McLaren, Karla. *The Language of Emotions: What Your Feelings Are Trying To Tell You.* Sounds True, Boulder, CO. 2010. 46,51.

McTaggart, Lynne. *The Intentional Experiment.* Free Press: A division of Simon & Schuster, Inc. 2007, 139, 155.

Moorjani, Anita. *Dying to Be Me: My Journey from Cancer, To Near Death, To True Healing.* Hay House, Inc. 2012. 139.

Nager and Shapiro. *The Bankstreet Approach. Early Childhood Education.* Developmental Interaction. http://en.wikipedia.org/wiki/Early-Childhood.edu.

National Institute of Health. *Misconceptions About Sleep.* A reprint from the National Institute of Heart, Lung, and Blood Institute. www.sleepdex.org/misconception.htm.

NurrieStearns, Mary LCSW, RYT and Rick NurrieStearns. *Yoga for Anxiety: Meditations and practices for calming the body and mind.* New Harbinger Publications, 2010. 24.

Olson, Lynn. *Supporting Teachers' Success.* Education Week, March 1, 2008. Published online: March 12, 2008.

Oreinstein, Peggy. *Should the World of Toys Be Gender-Free?* The New York Times. December 29, 2011. On line January 5, 2012. www.nytimes.com/2011/12/30opinion/does-stripping-gender-from-toys-really-make.

Partanen, Anu. *What Americans Keep Ignoring About Finland's School Success*. The Atlantic Monthly. Posted on line Dec 29, 2011. 3 p.m. 1529. www.theatlantic.com.

Perry, Rachel. *Developing Your Intuition Workshop*. Centerville Yoga and Wellness Center. Centerville, MA. June 2011. www.rachelperrymedium.com.

Pert, Candice. *Molecules of Emotion: The Science Behind Mind-Body Medicine*. Scribner, New York, NY. 1997, 135.

Pick, Marcelle, OB/GYN NP. *Deep Breathing: The truly essential exercise*. Posted April 20, 2011 on www.womentowomen.comfatigueandstress/deepbreathing. She is also the author of *Are you Tired and Wired?*

Pink, Daniel H. *A Whole New Mind: Why right brainers will rule the future*. Riverhead Books. Penguin Group. 2005, 1,2.

Powers, Sarah. *Insight Yoga*. Workshop held on July 27, & 28 2012 at The Church of Holy Christ, Orleans, M.A.

Pratt, George J. Ph.D. and Peter T. Lambrou, Ph.D. *Instant Emotional Healing: Acupressure for the Emotions*. Broadway Books a division of Ramdom House, 2006, 153.

Rathus, Spencer A. Psych, Second Edition. Wadsworth. Cengage Learning. Belmont, CA. 2009, p. 152.

Raymond Trevor Bradley, PH.D., Rollin McCraty, PH.D., Dana Tomasino, BA. *The Heart Has Its Own "Brain" and Consciousness*. Mindful Muscle. Institute of HeartMath's research and publications, 2011. www.mindfulmuscleblog.com/heart-has-consciousness.

Responsive Classroom, a researched backed approach to increasing academic achievement, improving social skills and decreasing behavior problems in elementary education. Resources for all teachers (including higher education) are available on the website www.responsiveclassroom.org.

Rochat, Philippe. *Five levels of self awareness as they unfold early in life.* Consciousness and Cognition 12, 2003, 717-731. Feb 27, 2003. Department of Psychology. Emory University, Atlanta, GA.www. psychology.emory.edu/cognition/ro. And www.sciencedirect.com.

Ronald E. Dahl, M.D. *The Consequences of Insufficient Sleep for Adolescents. Links between sleep and emotional regulation.* Phi Delta Kappan, vol. 80, No. 05, January 1999, 354-359.

Rosen, Richard. *The Yoga of Breath: A step by step guide to pranayama.* Shambhala, Boston & London, 2002. 22, 36, 102.

Ross, Steven. *Happy Yoga: 7 Reasons Why There's Nothing to Worry About.* Harper Collins, 2003, 249.

Ruiz, Don Miguel. *The Four Agreements: A practical guide to personal freedom.* Amber- Allen Publishing Company, San Rafael, CA. 1997.

Srerraman. *School Children Exposed to Fluorescent Lights Are At The Risk of Headaches.* Child Health News. Sept 6, 2007. www.medindia. net.

Simon-Thomas, Emiliana. *Compassion remains a gift of the spirit.* A consulting neuroscientist with Stanford University Center for Compassion and Altruism Research and Education. Quoted in The Yoga Journal, 81, August, 2012.

Simmons, Rachel. *The Curse of The Good Girl: Raising Authentic Girls with Courage and Confidence.* The Penguin Press, New York, 2009, 38.

Stoddard, David A. and Robert J. Tamsy. *The Heart of Mentoring: Ten Proven Principles for Developing People To Their Fullest Potential.* Nav Press, Colorado, Springs, CO. 2009. www.navpress.com.

Tierney, John. *A Serving of Gratitude May Save the Day.* Quoted Professor Nathan DeWall who led studies at The University of Kentucky. The New York Times, November 21, 2011.

Ward, Sarah, M.S., CCC/SLP. *A Practical Strategies Seminar Focusing on Organization and Self-Management Skills.* Center for Executive Function Skill Development. Cape Codder Resort, Hyannis, MA. March 26, 2011. www.executivefunctiontherapy.com.

Weintraub, Amy, MFA, RYT. Lifeforce Yoga Part 1. Cape Cod Institute. Cape Media Company, Brewster, MA.

Weintraub, Amy, MFA, RYT. *Yoga Skills for Therapists: Effective Practices for Mood Management.* WW. Norton & Company, Inc. 2012.

Williamson, Marianne. *A Return to Love: Reflections on the Principles Of A Course In Miracles.* Harper Collins, 1992, Xviii, 18.

Zachary, Lois J. *The Mentors Guide.* Jossey-Bass Inc. San Franciso, CA. 2000.

Zhivotovskaya, Emiliya. *Smile and Others Smile With You: Health Benefits, Emotional Contagion and Mimicry.* Sept 27, 2008. http://positivepsychologynews.com.

Zick, Ana. M.A., C.A.G.S. Licensed mental health and holistic counselor. Barnstable, MA. www.lotusheartcenter.com.

Additional Resources

Healy, Jane. M., PH.D. *Failure to Connect: How Computers Affect Our Children's Minds-for Better and Worse.* Simon & Schuster, New York, NY. 1998.

Small, Gary, M.D. and Gigi Vorgan. *iBrain: Surviving the technological alteration of the modern mind.* Harper Collins Publishers, New York, New York. 2008.

19375745R00135

Made in the USA
Lexington, KY
16 December 2012